PRESENTED TO

FROM

ON

THE PEACE TABLE: A STORYBOOK BIBLE
Copyright © 2023 by Herald Press, Harrisonburg, Virginia 22803, and Brethren Press, Elgin, Illinois 60120.
   All rights reserved.
Library of Congress Control Number: 2023934418
International Standard Book Number: 978-1-5138-1226-7
Printed in Canada.
Writers: Chrissie Muecke, Jasmin Pittman Morrell, Teresa Kim Pecinovsky
Editors: Chrissie Muecke, Joan L. Daggett, Rachel Nussbaum Eby
Front cover art: Erin Bennett Banks

To order or request information, visit ShineCurriculum.com.

27 26 25 24 23   10 9 8 7 6 5 4 3 2 1

the PEACE TABLE

A storybook BIBLE

SHINE
LIVING IN GOD'S LIGHT

Herald Press
Harrisonburg, Virginia

Brethren Press
Elgin, Illinois

Table of Contents

WELCOME

EXTRAS

OLD TESTAMENT STORIES

NEW TESTAMENT STORIES

Dear families,

What do you think of when you hear the word *peace*? The end of a conflict or war? A dove? A hug from a friend? A beautiful sunset? Yes! Peace is all these things and so much more. The Hebrew word *shalom* beautifully combines four aspects of peace: peace with God, ourselves, each other, and all creation.

Jesus is our best example of how to live as a peacemaker. He shared meals with friends and those who were rejected by society. He spent time alone praying. He healed people and valued children. He taught crowds using examples from nature. But Jesus also argued with religious leaders about difficult faith questions. He flipped over tables in the temple. He rejected greed and pride. He got angry. You may not associate those actions with peace. Yet they give us unexpected clues about how to live boldly as peacemakers.

What happens at *The Peace Table*? Here we retell ancient stories of people seeking to follow God, and often messing up. We sing songs, read poetry and prophecies, explore history, learn about laws and commandments, and even read other peoples' mail. But it is not just God's story from the Bible that we share here. We offer our own stories as well—our joys and struggles, our wisdom and mistakes, our favorite memories, and our desires for a better world. As we hold our stories in the light of God's story, we better understand who we are as individuals, families, and communities of faith.

Conversations around *The Peace Table* are not always easy. We come from many different places. We understand God's story in unique ways. We have different ideas, beliefs, values, and experiences. Yet, when we come together at this table, we discover anew that we are all beloved children of God, made in God's image. We learn from each other and grow together as peacemakers.

So, pull up a seat. Bring a friend and an enemy. Enjoy the compelling stories from *The Peace Table* and find inspiration in the beautiful artwork. Speak from the heart, ask hard questions, be curious, listen well, share your doubts, and pray together often. Be ready to eat, dance, sing, create, imagine, and wonder together. Consider how these ancient stories connect to the life of your family and community today. Then use your unique God-given gifts to help make a more peaceful, just, and beautiful world.

May God bless you richly with love, peace, and courage for the journey.

—Chrissie Muecke, Jasmin Pittman Morrell, and Teresa Kim Pecinovsky (authors)

> **For [Jesus] is our peace. He came and proclaimed peace to you who were far off and peace to those who were near.**
> —Ephesians 2:14a, 17 (NRSV)

Introduction to
The Peace Table: A Storybook Bible

BOOK CREATION PROCESS

The Peace Table was developed and created with the input of many people. A group of church leaders and seminary professors in the United States and Canada met to discern the list of stories, identify the peace paths, and address theological questions. A team of writers worked collaboratively to write 45 of the most challenging stories in the book. Others gave input about illustrations. Read more about the authors, theological advisors, and illustration consultants on pages 374–376.

> **And let the peace of Christ rule in your hearts, to which indeed you were called in the one body.**
>
> **–Colossians 3:15a (NRSV)**

BIBLE STORIES

Each Bible story in *The Peace Table* is a biblically faithful retelling. The stories do not include every detail of the scripture passages. As children grow, they will have opportunities to explore the full text in greater depth. For elementary children, the focus is on conveying the heart and spirit of each story in simple language that they can easily understand.

ILLUSTRATIONS

We hope that the illustrations inspire, surprise, challenge, and delight you. They were created by 30 illustrators from a range of backgrounds and locations, using many different artistic styles and mediums. Learn more about the illustrators on pages 376–382.

Some of the illustrations may be different than what you expect. Several are illustrated in settings around the world. This is not to suggest that the actual events happened in Indonesia, Mexico, Malaysia, or Canada. Rather, it is an invitation to imagine how the timeless and universal message of the Bible lives and breathes in our own families, churches, communities, and around the world.

Jesus has intentionally been depicted with a variety of appearances. In his book *The Faces of Jesus,* Reverend Frederick Buechner explores how a diversity of representations helps a diversity of people to understand the significance of Jesus' incarnation. Jesus was born as a Jewish child in a Middle Eastern family, so some illustrations show him with that appearance. But Jesus also transcends race and culture and is God incarnate ("God with us") for all people in all times and places. It is our prayer that when children see these varied representations of Jesus, they will more easily recognize the image of God within themselves and each other.

Using *The Peace Table*

In addition to a retelling of the Bible story, each spread has additional prompts to help you engage the Bible story with children. The following categories are found throughout the book:

Wonder & Share ☼

Every story includes wondering and discussion questions to help you go deeper into the story and its significance for your life.

Pray 💬

A prayer prompt is included with each story. This prompt sometimes references prayer content on pages 338–347, such as different types of prayer and interactive ways to pray.

Practice Peace 🕊

How can you live at peace with God, self, others, and creation? This prompt provides concrete ideas, often referencing the peace content on pages 348–355.

Peace Path 🏃

There are 12 peace paths throughout the book. Learn more about peace paths below and on page 16.

Dig In 📖

Bible background information, maps, and timelines will help children understand the context and setting of the Bible stories.

Live It ☀

These action-focused ideas will help you bring the message of the story into daily life.

Art Spotlight 🎨

Some illustrators included unique elements from places around the world, which are highlighted here.

These prompts are geared for a range of ages, so choose items that will work best for the current age of your child.

PEACE PATHS

On page 16, there are a series of peace paths. These paths allow you to choose your own adventure through the book! Each path has five stories from the Old and New Testaments that relate to a peacemaking theme. These themes explore the biblical concept of *shalom*: peace with God, self, others, and creation. A page number is provided for the first story in the path. For subsequent stories, look for the page number in the "Peace Path" section near the Bible story.

EXTRA MATERIALS

The Extras begin on page 338. A section on prayer includes descriptions of different types of prayers, interactive ways to pray, and finger prayer paths. A section on peacemaking devotes attention to the four aspects of *shalom*. There are also Old and New Testament timelines, the books of the Bible, maps, diagrams of the temples, and the events of Holy Week. A pronunciation guide is included on page 372 for the many challenging names and places in the Bible stories.

Seek peace and pursue it.

—1 Peter 3:11b (NRSV)

Peace Paths

Choose your own peace adventure! Pick a peace path to follow through the book. The starting page number for the first story in the path is shown below. After you read that Bible story, look for the next page number in the "Peace Path" section near the story. There is a little hand to point the way. Can you follow all the paths?

PEACE WITH GOD

God Welcomes All
(PAGE 30)
Hagar
Strong Sisters
Zacchaeus
The Road to Ethiopia
Good News for All

God's Spirit Moves
(PAGE 110)
A New King
Speak to the Bones
My Beloved Son
A Nighttime Visitor
Pentecost

God Is Amazing
(PAGE 60)
In the Wilderness
Bow or Burn
A Hungry Crowd
Lazarus, Come Out!
The Empty Tomb

PEACE INSIDE

I Am Special
(PAGE 88)
Song of Wonder
Written on Your Heart
Born in Bethlehem
Let the
Children Come
One Body, Many Gifts

I Need Comfort
(PAGE 114)
Fly like an Eagle
Song of Shelter
Birds and Flowers
Peace I Leave
with You
God Is Near

I Am Not Alone
(PAGE 86)
Song of a Shepherd
Lift the Valleys
The Good Shepherd
Parables of the Lost
Worthy Is the Lamb

PEACE WITH OTHERS

Love Your Enemies
(PAGE 40)
Isaac and His
Neighbors
Abigail's Idea
Swords and Plows
Love Your Enemies
Jesus Is Our Peace

Family Problems
(PAGE 28)
Lot's Choice
Jacob and Esau
Joseph the Dreamer
Mary and Martha
Parable of a Family

Love Your Neighbor
(PAGE 82)
King David's Table
Five Friends
Who Is My Neighbor?
Parable of the
Sheep and Goats
Daily Bread

PEACE WITH CREATION

Nature Trail
(PAGE 20)
God Creates
Wolves and Lambs
Job and the
Whirlwind
Parable of the
Mustard Seed
A New Creation

Let It Grow
(PAGE 44)
Prison to Palace
Jubilee
Ruth and Naomi
Song of Creation
Parable of the Sower

Water Wonders
(PAGE 58)
The Red Sea
The Promised Land
Cast Your Nets
Wedding Wonders
Storm at Sea

Children's Faith Development

A sense of love and belonging is very important for young children. Learning to communicate clearly, express feelings, show empathy, apologize, and forgive are all important areas of growth. Because young children are concrete thinkers, try to communicate faith concepts in ways that connect to their everyday, sensory experiences.

Over time, children perceive God as both creator and friend. They begin to value rules and fair play. Because they want good to win over evil, children may imagine God as a divine superhero who rewards good and punishes evil. They have a growing understanding of wrongdoing and forgiveness. They strongly desire to please adults and may feel guilt or shame when they do things that they know are wrong. It is therefore essential for adults to convey the unconditional love of God in tangible ways.

Older children want to know how God is at work in their lives and in the world. As they become increasingly aware of the larger issues of the world, they may show compassion and concern for those who are suffering or being treated unfairly. They may pose challenging questions about why difficult or painful things happen in the world. Older children respond to God in deeply personal ways. They express their feelings through art, prayer, silence, and faith conversations. In a safe and respectful environment, they can share their spiritual experiences with others. They are careful observers of the adults around them and need role models who live out their faith.

TALKING ABOUT DIFFICULT STORIES

The wondering questions included in this storybook Bible nurture curiosity and open-ended conversation. Rather than asking children to recall facts or details about the plot, wondering questions encourage children to imagine that they are part of the story. What would it have been like to see the newly created world? How did Mary feel when she held baby Jesus for the first time?

This style of questioning is particularly helpful for the challenging stories in the Bible. There aren't always easy answers, and it is okay to wonder together why people suffer or why bad things happen in the world. You can acknowledge that these things are hard to understand while *also* reassuring your child that God is always present with us.

Tip: Read each Bible story to yourself first. What might be potentially confusing or troubling to your child? Think about how you want to respond to the questions that may arise. It is okay to say, "I don't know. That is hard for me to understand too. Let's keep thinking and talking about it!"

> *Jesus said, "Blessed are the peacemakers, for they will be called children of God."*
> **—Matthew 5:9 (NRSV)**

OLD TESTAMENT

God Creates

GENESIS 1:1–2:3

WHEN BEGINNING, God created in the dark.
Earth and sky had no shape. God's Spirit fluttered over the water.

Then God said, "Let there be light."
Light shone. God saw the light was good.
God called the light Day, and the darkness Night.
There was nighttime and morning, the first day.

Then God said, "Let there be a dome."
A dome appeared, like a ceiling over the water.
God called the ceiling Sky.
There was nighttime and morning, the second day.

Then God said, "Let land appear."
And it did. God saw the land was good.
God called the dry land Earth, and the water around it Seas.
Then God said, "Let the Earth sprout plants and fruit trees."
Up sprouted every plant and tree. God saw goodness in what grew.
There was nighttime and morning, the third day.

Then God said, "Let there be lights in the sky."
The sun, moon, and stars arose, and God saw goodness.
There was nighttime and morning, the fourth day.

Then God said, "Let there be animals in the water, and birds in the sky."
Sea creatures swam. Birds soared across the sky.
God called them good and blessed them.
There was nighttime and morning, the fifth day.

Then God said, "Let there be animals on the land."
Wild animals and tame animals roamed. God called them good.
Then God said, "Let us make humans in our image to care for the earth."
And God created humans and blessed them.
God saw everything God made and agreed it was all very good.
There was nighttime and morning, the sixth day.

God finished creating. And on the seventh day, God rested.

Wonder & Share

▶ I wonder what sounds God heard each day of creation.

▶ Share an example of something you have created.

▶ You were created in the image of God! Look in a mirror and celebrate the special way you were made.

Pray

Gather things from nature, such as leaves, sticks, flowers, shells, pine cones, grass, and stones. Make a display, saying a prayer of thanks as you add each item.

Peace Path
Nature Trail

Find different parts of creation in the story illustration. Which do you like best? How can you care for and enjoy the world God made? Look at the "Peace with Creation" ideas on pages 354–355.

PAGE 116

In the Garden

GENESIS 3

GOD PLANTED A GARDEN in Eden and placed a man and a woman there to live. The trees were beautiful to see, and their branches held delightful fruits to eat. A river flowed from the garden, and animals of all kinds roamed the land.

A snake also lived in the garden. Out of all the wild animals God made, the snake was the most cunning.

The snake asked the woman, "Did God really tell you not to eat any of the fruit from these trees?"

"We can eat fruit from all the trees," she replied, "except the tree in the middle of the garden. God said we cannot eat or touch its fruit. If we do, we will die."

"You won't die," the snake told them. "God knows that if you eat the fruit, you will be like God. Then you'll judge right from wrong."

Eve looked at the tree's fruit. It looked delicious. She wanted to be like God, so she picked some fruit and ate it. The man ate some too.

Then Adam and Eve wanted to cover their bodies and hide. They tore leaves from a fig tree and tried to cover themselves. When they heard God's footsteps in the garden, they did not come out to greet God.

"Where are you?" God called.

The man said, "I heard you, and I was afraid to come out of hiding,"

"Why were you afraid?" God wondered. "Did you do what I asked you not to do?"

The man looked at the woman. "She gave me fruit from the tree, and I ate."

"Did you?" God asked the woman.

"The snake tricked me, and I ate," she said.

From then on, God made the snake crawl on its belly. Adam and Eve had to work hard to grow their own food. They had to leave the beautiful garden. But not before God sewed clothes for them, so they wouldn't feel like hiding from God.

Wonder & Share

▶ Imagine spending time with God in the beautiful garden.
▶ How did God care for Adam and Eve?
▶ Have you ever felt like hiding? Why?

Pray

Say an "I'm sorry" prayer, silently or aloud. This is called *confession*. Then use a strong voice to say, "God loves me no matter what!" Discover other ways to feel at peace with God on pages 348–349.

Dig In

Eden means "abundance, plenty, fullness." The Tigris and Euphrates rivers are named in the description of Eden in Genesis 2. Flowing through a vast desert, these two rivers still provide water for drinking, crops, and transportation today.

God's Promise to Creation

GENESIS 6:5–9:17

AS THE YEARS WENT ON, human beings began ruining the earth and all the good things God created. Violence spread. God's heart felt grief. This was not the world God desired.

Only Noah and his family continued to follow the ways of God. God said to Noah: "A flood will cover the whole earth with water. Everyone and everything will die, except you and your family, because you follow me. Build an ark out of cypress wood. Bring two of every kind of animal, bird, and insect into the ark. Bring enough food to feed all your family and the animals too." God promised to keep Noah safe. Noah did everything God asked him to do.

When Noah, his family, and all the animals and creatures were safely in the ark, the rain began to fall. It rained for 40 days and 40 nights. Water flooded everything.

When the rain finally stopped and the flood waters drained away, God told Noah to open the ark's door. Noah looked out and saw dry land. Noah, his family, and all the animals and creatures left the ark. Noah built an altar to honor God.

God felt pleased and wanted the earth to be filled with people and animals again. So, God made a covenant—a holy promise for all of creation. God said,

> "Never again will a flood destroy the earth.
> As long as the earth lasts,
> seedtime and harvest, cold and heat,
> summer and winter, day and night
> will not end."

As a sign of the covenant, God painted a rainbow in the sky.

Wonder & Share

▸ I wonder how Noah felt when God told him about the coming flood.
▸ I wonder how we can help protect the earth.
▸ Share ideas for how to care for pets, wild animals, and endangered species.

Pray

Praise God with color prayers. Start with red. Name red things that you want to praise God for, then continue with orange, yellow, green, blue, purple, brown, black, white—and any other colors you like!

Dig In 📖

The ark was as long as one and a half football fields! It had a lower, middle, and upper deck. Pitch was used to make it watertight. Turn to page 50 to read about another "boat" covered with pitch.

Abram and Sarai

GENESIS 12:1–9

ONE OF NOAH'S DESCENDANTS was named Abram. Abram, his wife Sarai, and his nephew Lot lived in Haran. It was a beautiful place, with a flowing river and good land for growing crops.

God spoke to Abram and said, "Leave your home, your country, and your people. Go to the land I will show you. I will make you a great nation. I will bless you, and you will bless others."

Abram, Sarai, and Lot packed everything they owned—their tents, blankets, food, and clothing. They rounded up their sheep, goats, donkeys, and cattle. Then they set out, leaving behind the life they knew.

For many weeks, Abram, Sarai, and Lot traveled. They walked and rode, talked and were silent. They got tired and rested. They cooked and ate together, remembering all they had seen each day.

Their journey took them past the Great Sea and the Jordan River. They went through the hill country into the land of Canaan, as far as the great tree of Moreh at Shechem. God appeared to Abram there, saying, "I will give this land to your children and grandchildren." How could this be? There were already many people living there, and Abram and Sarai had no children. Abram built an altar there to God.

Then Abram, Sarai, and Lot traveled toward the hills east of Bethel. They put up their tents and built another altar, calling on the name of God.

Wonder & Share 💡

▶ I wonder how Sarai felt about leaving her home and friends.

▶ Abram built an altar to worship God. What could you create to show love for God?

Pray 💬

People leave their homes for many reasons. Sometimes a parent gets a new job and the family must move. People move closer to friends and family. But sometimes people are forced to leave. Pray for those who have left home due to natural disasters, danger, or war.

Practice Peace 🕊️

God told Abram and Sarai that they would be a blessing to others. What loving things could you say or do to bless your family, friends, and neighbors?

Lot's Choice

GENESIS 13

ABRAM AND SARAI BECAME VERY RICH. They had lots of silver and gold and many herds of animals. Their nephew Lot also had many flocks, herds, and tents.

They traveled together back to the land of Bethel, but there was not enough food and water for all their animals. Abram and Sarai's herders began to fight with Lot's herders. Both groups needed the grazing land and water, or their animals would die.

So Abram said, "Lot, we are family. Let there be peace between us and peace between our herders. Look at this land, to the left and right. Choose one area for your family and herds. After you choose, I will take the other land for my family."

Lot looked around. He saw the plain of the Jordan to the east. It was well-watered, like the garden of God and the land of Egypt. He chose that land and moved his family and herds there.

Abram and Sarai set up their tents in the land of Canaan. God said, "Look north, south, east, and west. I will give all the land you see to your children and grandchildren. Your descendants will be like the dust of the earth—too many to be counted. Travel the length and breadth of this land that I will give you."

So Abram and Sarai set out again. They went to Hebron and settled by the oaks of Mamre, building an altar to God.

Wonder & Share

▶ I wonder how Abram felt about giving Lot the first choice.
▶ Name three things you like about where you live. If you could choose a new home, where would you go?

Pray 💬

God told Abram and Sarai to travel over the whole land. Turn to page 346 and use your finger to slowly trace the prayer path as you pray.

Peace Path
Family Problems

Does your family ever fight over "stuff" like toys or snacks? Does it ever seem like there isn't enough for everyone? How did Abram and Lot handle this problem? What can you do? Look at the "Peace with Others" ideas on pages 352–353.

✍ **PAGE 34**

Hagar

GENESIS 16, 21

HAGAR WAS BORN IN EGYPT and was enslaved by Abram and his wife Sarai. Hagar had to do anything Sarai told her to do.

In her old age, Sarai didn't have the one thing she wanted most: a child. God had promised to give her a son, but it still hadn't happened. So Sarai said to Abram, "Take Hagar as another wife so that she can have a son for us." Abram agreed. Hagar had no choice.

After Hagar became pregnant, Sarai treated her so badly that Hagar ran away into the Wilderness of Shur. An angel came to her and asked, "Where have you come from and where are you going?" Hagar told the angel what Sarai had done. "Go back to Sarai and Abram," the angel told Hagar. "You will have a son named Ishmael. Your descendants will be too many to count." Hagar gave God a new name: *El Roi,* which means "God who sees." Then she returned home and gave birth to her son, Ishmael.

Years later, Sarai finally gave birth to her own son, just as God had promised. She named him Isaac. One day Hagar's teenage son Ishmael was playing with Isaac, who was just a young boy. Sarai's anger at Hagar burned stronger than ever. She said to Abram, "Send Hagar and Ishmael into the wilderness." Abram was distressed; he loved Ishmael. But he did what Sarai said and sent them into the wilderness.

Soon Hagar and Ishmael's water ran out. What could they do? Ishmael was dying from thirst.

Hagar laid him under a bush for shade. Then she went a short distance away and cried out to God. An angel said to her, "Don't be afraid. God has heard your cries and the voice of your son." God showed her and Ishmael a well of water and promised to always take care of Ishmael and Hagar.

Wonder & Share

▶ Sarai means "princess." Abram means "high father." Hagar means "the foreigner." Ishmael means "God hears." Isaac means "laughter." How do their names help us understand this story better?

▶ Share about a time you felt hopeless, scared, or lonely. Who or what helped you?

Pray

Hagar gave God a new name: God Who Sees. Pray using that name for God. Then choose another name for God and use it in your prayer.

Peace Path
God Welcomes All

Abram and Sarai sent Hagar into the wilderness, where she and Ishmael could have easily died. How did God respond to Hagar? What could you do for someone who is rejected or treated harshly?

▶ PAGE 66

A Promised Child

GENESIS 17, 18, 21

WHEN ABRAM WAS 99 YEARS OLD, God appeared to him again. God made a covenant with Abram—a holy promise. God said, "Obey me and be trustworthy. Then I will make you a great nation and give you the land of Canaan. Your name will now be Abraham. Sarai's name will now be Sarah. I will bless Sarah and give her a son. Name him Isaac."

Abraham bowed down to the ground and laughed. How could he and Sarah have a baby when he was 99 years old and she was 90?

One hot summer afternoon, Abraham saw three visitors standing near his tent. He brought water so they could wash their feet. He and Sarah quickly prepared a meal of fresh bread, meat, yogurt, and milk for them.

As the visitors ate, Sarah listened at the tent flap. She overhead one of them say, "Your wife Sarah will have a son." It was the Lord speaking.

Sarah laughed. She was old. How could she have a baby? The Lord said, "Why did Sarah laugh? Nothing is too hard for God."

It happened as God said. Sarah gave birth to a son. Abraham named him Isaac, which means "laughter." Sarah said, "God has brought laughter for me! Whoever hears of Isaac's birth will laugh with me. For I have given birth to a son in my old age."

Wonder & Share 🔆

▶ I wonder why God changed Abram and Sarai's names. What new name would you choose for yourself?
▶ What is something seemingly impossible that you would like God to do?

Pray 💬

Isaac means "laughter." Say a joyful prayer! Dance or wave a scarf, ribbon, or piece of cloth as you pray.

Dig In 📖

God promised to give Abraham and Sarah the land of Canaan. Find Canaan on the map on page 362.

Jacob and Esau

GENESIS 25, 27, 32, 33

ABRAHAM AND SARAH'S SON Isaac grew up and married Rebekah. She became pregnant with twins and gave birth to Esau first, then to Jacob. Esau grew up to be a skilled hunter. This pleased his father because Isaac loved to eat meat. Jacob was a quiet man who stayed near the tents. This pleased his mother, Rebekah. She loved Jacob best.

One day Jacob was cooking stew. Esau came in from hunting and was so hungry that he felt like he was dying. "Jacob, let me have some of that stew," he begged.

But Jacob did not share it freely. Instead, he said, "First you have to sell me your birthright."

Esau paused. If he sold his birthright, he would lose the double inheritance and would not be the family leader after his father's death. But Esau was desperate for food, so he sold his birthright.

Only then did Jacob give him bread and lentil stew.

When Isaac was very old, he could no longer see. He called his son Esau to him. "My son, I am old, and I will die soon. Go out into the field and hunt. Bring me my favorite meal and then I will give you the blessing for the oldest child." So Esau took his bow and arrows and went away.

Rebekah had been listening. Even though Jacob was the younger child, she wanted him to have that blessing instead of Esau. She called Jacob. "Quick!" she told him. "Go and get two goats. I will prepare them just like your father likes. Then you can take the food to him, and he will bless you."

Jacob did this. Rebekah put Esau's best robe on Jacob, covering his arms with animal skin to make them feel like Esau's hairy arms. Jacob took the food to his father. Isaac hesitated. Was this really Esau? But Jacob assured him with a lie, "Yes, I am your oldest son." So Isaac blessed him, even though he was the younger son. Jacob hurried away.

Just then Esau returned from hunting and brought food to his father. Isaac was confused. Who was this? How could it be Esau? He had given away Esau's blessing already. Esau cried out bitterly, "Bless me too, father!" But Isaac could not. Esau wept.

Esau hated Jacob because of what he had done. Esau said to himself, "Once my father is dead, I will kill my brother."

Rebekah learned of Esau's plan to kill Jacob, so she sent Jacob away to her brother's home in Haran. In Haran, Jacob married and became very rich. Twenty years later, Jacob decided he wanted to go home. He set out, but he soon heard that his brother Esau was coming toward him with 400 men. Terrified, he divided his family and flocks and herds into two different groups and sent them in separate directions. He prayed, "God, I am not worthy of your steadfast love and faithfulness. But please save me from my brother's fury."

Jacob sent animals as gifts to his brother—200 goats, 200 sheep, 30 camels, 50 cows, and 30 donkeys. Maybe this would keep his brother from attacking him.

The next day, Esau approached with his men. Jacob went toward him, bowing to the ground seven times. But Esau did not attack! Esau ran to meet Jacob and hugged him instead! He kissed him and they wept together. Jacob said, "Seeing your face is like seeing the face of God."

Jacob introduced Esau to his family for the first time. Then they went their separate ways in peace.

Wonder & Share 💡

▶ I wonder how Jacob felt about pretending to be Esau.
▶ I wonder what changed Esau's mind about killing his brother.
▶ Share about a time you felt angry at a friend or someone in your family. What can happen if we hold onto our anger?

Pray 💬

Say a prayer of blessing for someone in your family. Use your own words or this blessing: "May God give you peace."

Peace Path 🌄
Family Problems

It was not just Jacob and Esau who made mistakes in this story. What could the parents, Isaac and Rebekah, have done differently? Talk as a family about times you have hurt one another. How can you show that you love each other?

 PAGE 42

Isaac and His Neighbors

GENESIS 26:12–33

ISAAC AND REBEKAH'S LAND produced huge crops. They had many flocks of animals and grew richer and richer. Their neighbors were jealous of them and filled their wells with dirt. King Abimelech told Isaac, "You must move. You are becoming too powerful."

Isaac and his family moved to the valley of Gerar and dug again the wells his father, Abraham, had dug years ago. But other people lived in this land, and they needed water too. They argued, "This water is ours!" So Isaac dug a different well. Again, the nearby herders argued over the water. So Isaac moved away and dug a new well. This time no one argued about it, so he named it Rehoboth and said, "God has made room for us."

Next, Isaac's family went to Beersheba. God appeared to Isaac in a dream there and said, "Do not be afraid. I am with you. I will bless you and give you a large family, just as I promised your father Abraham." Isaac built an altar to God and had his servants dig a new well.

King Abimelech and the commander of his army followed Isaac to Beersheba. Isaac said to them, "Why are you coming here now? You hate me and you sent me away."

The king replied, "We see that the Lord is with you. Let us not argue over land and wells anymore. Let us agree to make peace with one another." They both promised and Isaac shared a great feast with them.

After the king left, Isaac's servants discovered water in the well they had dug. Isaac called it Shibah, which means "promise."

Wonder & Share

▶ I wonder how King Abimelech could tell that God was with Isaac.

▶ I wonder if Isaac and the king kept their peace promise.

▶ Share about a time you argued with someone. How did you work it out?

Pray

Fill a pitcher with water. Slowly pour a glass of water for the person next to you as you pray for that person. After everyone's glass is full, drink the water together.

Peace Path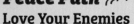
Love Your Enemies

Isaac and his family chose to move away rather than fight over the wells. When is it important to stay and work through a problem, and when should you leave a situation?

PAGE 80

Joseph the Dreamer

GENESIS 37

ISAAC'S SON JACOB lived in the land of Canaan. Jacob had many children, but Joseph was his favorite. When Joseph was 17 years old, his father presented him with a fancy coat as a sign of his love. The brothers hated Joseph for it and could not be kind to him. In turn, Joseph told his father bad things about his brothers.

Joseph had a dream and told it to his brothers. "We were working in a field," he said. "My bundle of wheat stood up. Your bundles of wheat bowed down to my bundle."

His brothers scoffed, "Do you really think you are going to be a king over us?" They hated him even more.

Joseph had another dream and could not resist telling his family: "The sun, moon, and 11 stars bowed down to me." Anger and jealousy rippled through the family.

One day, Jacob sent Joseph out to the fields in search of his brothers, who were watching the sheep. When they saw him coming, they plotted together, saying, "Let's kill him! Then we will see what happens to his dreams."

But one brother, Reuben, stepped in and said, "No! Do not kill him! Throw him into a pit in the wilderness, but do not hurt him." Reuben planned to sneak back later and rescue Joseph. The brothers agreed. They grabbed Joseph, stripped him of his coat, and threw him into a pit.

Soon some Ishmaelite travelers came by on their way to Egypt. Another brother, Judah, said, "What do we gain by killing our brother? Let's sell him to the travelers instead." So they sold Joseph for 20 pieces of silver, and he was taken to Egypt.

The brothers put animal's blood on Joseph's coat and took it to their father, Jacob, making him think Joseph was dead. Jacob wept and tore his clothes.

Meanwhile, the travelers sold Joseph to Potiphar, who worked for the king of Egypt.

Wonder & Share ☼

▶ Look at each picture of Joseph. I wonder how he felt.
▶ Share about a time you said "no" to something that was wrong, like Reuben did.

Pray 💬

Pray a "help me" prayer, telling God a problem, fear, or need you have.

Peace Path ⛰

Family Problems

What choices did the brothers consider when Joseph came to the field to find them? What else could they have done? Look at "Peace with Others" on pages 352–353 for ideas.

☞ PAGE 232

Prison to Palace

GENESIS 39–41

AFTER HIS BROTHERS SOLD HIM, Joseph was enslaved by Potiphar in Egypt. Joseph worked very hard, but Potiphar's wife told lies about him and had him thrown into prison. God was with Joseph and showed him great love.

A servant of the king was also sent to prison. One morning, Joseph saw that the servant was upset because of a dream he had. After helping him understand the dream, Joseph said, "Please remember me when you are set free. Say something to the king so that I can be free too." But the servant forgot.

Two years later, the king of Egypt had two strange dreams. In the first, seven skinny cows came out of the Nile River and ate seven fat cows. In the second dream, seven thin heads of grain swallowed seven full heads of grain. What did these dreams mean? The king's magicians did not know.

The king's servant finally remembered Joseph. He said to the king, "When I was in prison, Joseph told me the meaning of my dream. Maybe he can help you." The king sent for Joseph.

After hearing the king's dreams, Joseph said, "The dreams mean that Egypt will have seven years with plenty of food and then seven years of a terrible famine when no food will grow. Choose someone wise to oversee the gathering and storage of food during the good years. Then there will be food to eat during the famine."

The king saw that Joseph was wise. He put Joseph in charge of the whole land of Egypt and gave Joseph his ring and fine clothes. At 30 years old, it was Joseph's job to get ready for the famine.

For seven years, Joseph gathered and stored grain. The grain was like the sand of the sea—too much to count. Then came seven years of famine. People were starving. They came from many countries to get food in Egypt. They begged for bread and Joseph sold them grain.

Wonder & Share

▶ I wonder how Joseph felt about being in prison for something he did not do.
▶ If it was your job to feed a large group of hungry people, how would you do it?
▶ Share about a time you were a leader.

Pray 💬

Joseph was a leader with an important job. Pray for leaders in your church, school, community, and country. What good things do you hope they will do?

Peace Path

Let It Grow

The earth produced so much grain that it was like the sand of the sea! Some people have more food than they need. Other people struggle to get enough to eat. What can be done about this problem?

PAGE 64

Family Reunion

GENESIS 42-46

THERE WAS A TERRIBLE FAMINE in Canaan, where Jacob's family was living. They desperately needed food. Jacob sent 10 of his sons to Egypt to buy grain. He kept his youngest son, Benjamin, at home.

In Egypt, the brothers went to see the governor who was selling the food. They bowed low in front of him. They did not know he was their brother Joseph.

Joseph was angry and pretended not to know his brothers. He said coldly, "You are spies." The brothers protested; they had only come to buy grain, leaving their father and younger brother Benjamin at home.

Joseph replied, "I will test you to see if this is true. I will give you grain, but one brother must stay in jail here. The rest of you go home and bring back Benjamin."

When the brothers returned with Benjamin, Joseph was full of emotion. He served them a meal, still not telling them who he was.

Joseph sent the brothers home again with more grain. This time he secretly hid his silver goblet and some silver in Benjamin's bag. When they left the city, Joseph sent a servant to arrest them as thieves.

The servant brought the brothers back. Joseph finally told them the truth: "I am Joseph," he said, crying loudly. The brothers were afraid because of what they had done to Joseph. But Joseph said, "Don't worry or blame yourselves for what you did. God sent me here to save many lives."

The brothers hugged and cried. Joseph said, "This famine will last for five more years. Go home, gather your family and animals, and come back to live with me."

The brothers went home with wagons full of food. They told their father, "Joseph is alive! He is leader over Egypt!" Jacob was amazed. The whole family went to Egypt. Joseph came out to meet them. Joseph threw his arms around his father and cried for a long time.

Wonder & Share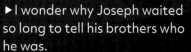

▶ I wonder why Joseph waited so long to tell his brothers who he was.

▶ Look back at Joseph's dreams on page 42. How did they come true in this story?

Pray 💬

Pray a "mix and match" prayer: Choose a type of prayer from pages 338–339 that relates to this Bible story. Then choose a creative way to pray your prayer from pages 340–341.

Practice Peace 🕊

What feelings did Joseph have toward his brothers throughout the story? If you are angry or frustrated with others, how do you calm down? Try one of the "Peace Inside" ideas on pages 350–351 this week.

Brave Midwives

EXODUS 1

AFTER MOVING TO EGYPT, Jacob's family grew and grew. There were children, parents, grandparents, aunts, uncles, and cousins everywhere! They called themselves the family of Israel.

Many years passed, and the Egyptians forgot how Joseph helped them during the famine. A new king called a Pharaoh ruled. He saw the Israelite people becoming a mighty people—just as God had promised Abraham. Pharaoh was afraid this huge family might one day rise up against the Egyptians. So he enslaved them. He forced them to make countless bricks to build his cities. They had to work long days in the fields without pay. He made their lives miserable. And yet, the family of Israel continued to grow.

Pharaoh had to put a stop to it. He called in two Israelite women named Shiphrah and Puah. They were midwives who went into homes to help deliver babies. Pharaoh told them, "When you deliver a Hebrew baby, you must kill all the boys and let only the girls live."

Shiphrah and Puah believed in the God of Israel and did not do what Pharaoh said. They kept delivering all the babies safely. Sometime later, Pharaoh found out that the family of Israel continued to grow bigger and stronger. He called Shiphrah and Puah back and said, "Why haven't you done what I commanded?"

The women tricked Pharaoh, saying, "The Israelite women are different than Egyptian women. They give birth by themselves before we even arrive."

And so the family of Israel continued to grow and grow. God blessed the midwives and made them the trusted leaders of their own households and families.

Wonder & Share

▶ What words would you use to describe the midwives?

▶ I wonder how long it was before Pharaoh realized the midwives had disobeyed his order.

▶ Share about a time you did something brave.

Pray

Babies are precious to God! Pretend to hold a baby as you pray for the babies you know or for babies around the world. Pray that they will be safe, healthy, and loved.

Dig In 📖

In Genesis 32:28, God gave Jacob the new name "Israel." That's why the descendants of Jacob were known as Israelites. Pharaoh called them "Hebrews," his way of saying that they were foreigners who did not belong in Egypt.

Baby in a Basket

EXODUS 1:22–2:10

WHEN THE MIDWIVES Shiphrah and Puah refused to kill the baby boys at birth, Pharaoh gave a command to everyone: Every boy that is born to a Hebrew woman must be thrown into the Nile River.

A Hebrew woman named Jochebed was about to give birth. Would she have a boy? Would the baby be safe? She gave birth to a son. Quickly the family hid the baby. They had to keep him very quiet. His sister Miriam rocked him when he cried and sang peaceful songs to help him sleep.

Day after day, week after week, they did all they could to keep him safe. But after three months, it wasn't possible to hide the baby anymore. So Jochebed wove a basket and coated it with pitch, which would keep the water out. She laid the baby in it and placed the basket among the reeds on the bank of the river. Miriam watched over her brother from a distance.

Pharaoh's daughter came down to the river to bathe. She saw the basket in the reeds and sent her maids to get it. She opened it and saw the baby. He was crying. Her heart filled with love and sadness. "This must be one of the Hebrew babies," she said.

Suddenly, Miriam had an idea. She came to Pharaoh's daughter and said, "Would you like me to find a Hebrew woman to nurse the baby for you?" Yes, that was a good plan.

So Miriam went home quickly and got her mother. They hurried back to Pharaoh's daughter, who said, "Take care of this baby for me. I will pay you. When he is grown up, bring him back to me, and I will adopt him as my son. I will name him Moses because I drew him out of the water."

Wonder & Share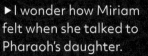

▸ I wonder how Miriam felt when she talked to Pharaoh's daughter.

▸ Share about a time that you felt both love and sadness for someone.

Pray 💬

Use play dough, clay, or paper and tape to form a basket shape. Write or draw your prayers on small pieces of paper, roll them up, and place them in your prayer basket.

Dig In 📖

Pitch is a black, sticky substance that is also called tar. Large amounts of pitch were found in pits near the Dead Sea. Pitch was used to coat things like boats to make them watertight.

Burning Bush

EXODUS 3:1–4:17

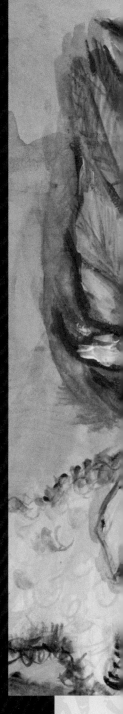

WHEN MOSES GREW UP, he became a shepherd. He led his sheep to places where they could graze. He found streams of water so they could drink. He protected them from wild animals. One day Moses and his flock came to Mount Horeb. A flame blazed from a bush, but the bush was not burned up. It was God's angel. Moses went to the bush. God called out, "Moses, Moses."

"Here I am," said Moses.

"Don't come any closer. Take off your sandals. This is special, holy ground. I am the God of Abraham and Sarah, of Isaac and Rebekah, of Jacob and Rachel."

Moses hid his face. He was afraid to look at God.

God said, "I have seen the pain and misery of my people in Egypt. I have heard their cries. I feel their suffering. I am sending you to Pharaoh to free my beloved people and bring them to a new land flowing with milk and honey."

"Me?" asked Moses. "Who am I to do this? The people won't believe me or listen to me. They will ask who sent me."

God said, "Tell them 'I Am Who I Am' sent you. I will be with you. Watch what I can do. Throw your staff on the ground."

When Moses did this, the staff turned into a snake. When he picked it up again, it turned back into a staff. God told him to put his hand inside his cloak. When he did, his hand had a disease. Then God healed it.

These signs were amazing. But Moses still wasn't sure. He said, "My mouth and tongue don't work like other people's. When I try to speak, my words do not come out right."

God replied, "I will teach you what you are to say. And I will send your brother Aaron with you so he can also speak." Moses took his staff and set off for Egypt.

Wonder & Share ☼

▶ I wonder how God feels about the bad things that happen in our lives.

▶ Share something you can do easily. What else is still hard for you?

Pray 💬

Find a special place inside or outside. Take off your shoes. Begin your prayer with Moses' words: "God, here I am."

Dig In 📖

Mount Horeb is also known as Mount Sinai. Find it on the map on page 362. It is located on the Sinai Peninsula in Egypt. This is the same mountain where God later gave Moses the Ten Commandments. Read about that on page 62.

Let My People Go

EXODUS 7:1–12:42

MOSES AND AARON went to Pharaoh and said, "This is what God says: 'Let my people go, so they may worship me in the wilderness.'" Pharaoh's heart was hard. He would not let them go.

So at God's command, Moses struck the water of the Nile River with his staff, and it turned to blood. But Pharaoh's magicians could do the same thing, so Pharaoh would not let the people go.

Again, Moses went to Pharaoh and said, "This is what God says: 'Let my people go, or frogs will cover the whole land.'" Pharaoh refused. Frogs swarmed the palace, the beds, the ovens, and even the kitchen bowls. But Pharaoh's magicians could do the same thing.

Pharaoh told Moses, "Pray to God. If God takes away the frogs, I will let you go." Moses prayed and the frogs died. But when Pharaoh saw that the frogs were no more, he changed his mind.

Again, Moses told Pharaoh to free the people. When he would not, Aaron raised his staff, and the dust of the earth be-came gnats and covered the whole land. Pharaoh's magicians could not do this. They told Pharaoh, "This is the hand of God." But he would not listen.

The next day, swarms of flies filled Egypt. But this time, the land of Goshen where the Israelites lived did not have any flies.

God said to Moses, "I will continue to show Pharaoh my great power until he frees my beloved people."

An awful disease came, and all the horses, camels, flocks, and herds of Egypt died. People and animals got painful boils on their skin. Hail fell on the land, destroying plants, crops, and trees. Locusts filled the houses and covered every surface of the land. There was a thick darkness in all of Egypt for three days. Yet Pharaoh's heart was not swayed by any of these terrible things. He refused to let the people go.

Moses warned Pharaoh, "All the firstborn people and animals in Egypt will die." But still Pharaoh refused to listen.

God told Moses what the Israelites should do. They were to mark their doorposts with lamb's blood. They should roast the lamb and eat it with bitter herbs and flatbread. They were to eat quickly, with their sandals on and their clothes ready for travel.

At midnight, all the firstborn in every unmarked home in Egypt died. Agonizing cries filled the land because someone was dead in every home. Even Pharaoh's own son died. Pharaoh called Moses and said, "Take everything and leave. Go worship your God."

Thousands of Israelites left, taking their bread dough before it could rise. They left with gold, silver, and clothing given to them by the Egyptians. Moses said, "Remember this day. Celebrate with a Passover feast every year, for God's great power has brought us out of slavery in Egypt."

Wonder & Share

▶ I wonder why it was so important to God to free the people of Israel.
▶ Which part of the story is most difficult or troubling to you? Where do you see signs of hope?

Pray

Create a feelings prayer using this pattern: name for God + feeling + request. For instance, *"God my Shepherd, I feel scared. Help me to know you are always with me."*

Practice Peace

What do you think it means to have a "hard heart"? What can happen when we stop caring about the pain of others? This week, notice when people are feeling sad or upset. Ask what they need. Maybe you can help.

The Red Sea

EXODUS 13:17–15:21

GOD LED THE ISRAELITES OUT OF EGYPT, through the wilderness, and toward the Red Sea. God went in front of them in a pillar of cloud by day. At night, God lighted their way in a pillar of fire.

When Pharaoh realized that the Israelites were truly gone, he said, "Why did I let them go? Who will build my cities and harvest my crops? I need slaves for that work." Pharaoh led 600 chariots and officers into the wilderness to recapture the Israelites.

When Pharaoh and his army drew close, the Israelites looked back in terror. They cried out to Moses, "Why did you bring us out of Egypt to die? It would have been better to work as slaves than to die in the wilderness."

Moses said, "Do not be afraid. Be still and see what God will do."

The pillar of cloud moved between the Israelites and Pharaoh's army. God told Moses to stretch out his staff over the sea. When Moses did, a great wind blew, parting the waters so that the people could walk through on dry ground.

Then the Egyptian army pursued them into the sea. God said to Moses, "Stretch out your staff over the sea." When he did, the waters rushed back. The dry path through the sea was gone. The whole army drowned.

When Moses and the Israelites realized that their suffering at the hands of Pharaoh was finally over, they sang a song to God.

"I will praise you, God, my strength.
    The enemy said, 'I will destroy you,'
but you led your people to safety.
    Who is like you?
You do awesome wonders!"

The prophet Miriam and all the women played tambourines and danced. They sang:

"Sing to the Lord,
    who has triumphed gloriously!
The horse and rider
    were thrown into the sea."

Wonder & Share

▶ Imagine walking through the sea, with a wall of water on each side of you!

▶ Find the emotions in this story. What sad, scary, happy, amazing, and confusing things happened? How did you feel during the story?

Pray

Moses told the people to be still and see what God would do. Take a few moments to be still and quiet. How was God at work in your life, your family, your community, or the world this week? Sing or dance to express praise to God, just like the Israelites did.

Peace Path

Water Wonders

In what ways was water important in this story? What are other examples of water being helpful or causing harm?

☞ **PAGE 68**

In the Wilderness

EXODUS 15:22–16:36

GOD HAD FREED THE ISRAELITES from slavery in Egypt, but their joy did not last long. After crossing the Red Sea, the people went into the Wilderness of Shur. It was hot and barren, and they could not find good water. They murmured against Moses, saying, "What are we going to drink?"

Moses cried out to God. God said, "Throw a piece of wood into the bitter water." Moses did, and the water became good to drink.

The people camped at Elim, an oasis in the desert with 12 springs of water and 70 date palm trees.

Leaving Elim, they entered the Wilderness of Sin. The people murmured against Moses again. "We wish God had killed us in Egypt. We are going to starve out here! At least in Egypt we had bread and meat."

God told Moses, "I will send down quail in the evening and bread in the morning. The people should gather only what they need for that day."

In the morning, thin flakes covered the ground. The people had never seen anything like it. "What is it?" they asked. Moses said, "This is the bread from God." The people called the food "manna." It tasted like wafers made with honey. They gathered enough for each person, just as God had said.

But some people gathered too much and saved it for the next day. In the morning, worms crawled through the manna, and it smelled bad.

God said, "On the sixth day, gather twice as much food so that you can rest on the Sabbath. Save two quarts of manna forever so that your children and grandchildren can see how I fed you." The people did as God said. The Israelites ate manna and quail for 40 years until they came to the land of Canaan.

Wonder & Share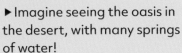

▶ Imagine seeing the oasis in the desert, with many springs of water!

▶ I wonder why God told the people to gather food for only one or two days at a time.

▶ If you could only eat two foods for 40 years, what would you choose?

Pray 💬

Say or sing a prayer before eating snacks and meals this week. Try one of the meal prayers on page 344.

Peace Path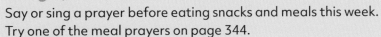

God Is Amazing

Trace the journey of the Israelites on the map on page 362. What amazing things did God do in each place? What does this show about God?

🪱 **PAGE 122**

On Mount Sinai

EXODUS 19:1–20:21; DEUTERONOMY 6:1–9

IN THE WILDERNESS, the Israelites came to Mount Sinai. God gave Moses a message for the people: "I am the Holy One who freed you from your suffering in Egypt, like a great eagle who sweeps up its young who cannot fly. I will make a covenant—a holy promise—with you. You must follow my ways and keep this covenant so you will be my most treasured people." The people agreed to follow God's covenant together.

Again God appeared to Moses and said, "Tell the people to get ready. On the third day I will come down upon the mountain." Moses and the people did as God said.

On the third day, thunder rumbled, lightning flashed, smoke billowed, the mountain trembled, and the blast of a trumpet sounded. Then it happened. God came! The whole earth announced the awesome arrival of God.

God told Moses how the Israelites were to live:

"I am the eternal and holy one, the only true God you must follow.
You must not create idols to worship.
My holy name shall not be used to make false promises.
Remember to have a sabbath day of rest.
Honor and respect your parents.
Do not murder.
Be faithful to your marriage.
Do not steal.
Do not lie about your neighbors.
Do not covet what belongs to others."

Later, God gave the Israelites a prayer for daily living and worship: **"Hear, O Israel, the Lord is our God, the Lord alone. You shall love the Lord your God with all your heart, and with all your soul, and with all your might.** Wherever you go, whatever you do, recite these words, live these words, and teach them to your children."

Wonder & Share

▶ Imagine seeing, hearing, and feeling God's presence at Mount Sinai.

▶ Share ideas for how to love God with your whole self.

Pray

The Shema is an important prayer that is in bold print in the Bible story. Pray the Shema morning and night, as the Israelites did.

Dig In

The instructions God gave at Mount Sinai are called the Ten Commandments. They show us how to love God and each other. God wrote them on tablets of stone, which were later placed in the Ark of the Covenant.

Jubilee

LEVITICUS 25

▸

GOD GAVE MOSES ANOTHER MESSAGE on Mount Sinai. God said, "When you come into the land I will give you, treat the land and each other in new ways. Gather food from the fields and vineyards for six years. But every seventh year, do not work the land. Let it rest, just like you rest for the Sabbath. I will provide food for you in that year.

After 49 years there will be a year of jubilee—a time of holy celebration and freedom. Play your trumpets throughout the land. Free the people who have unpaid debts. Forgive them what they owe. Jubilee is a reminder not to cheat others of their land or money. If someone is poor and needs food and money to survive, do not use their need to make yourself rich.

I am the Holy One who brought you out of Egypt. If strangers and foreigners come to the land, you must treat them with fairness and compassion. Remember: you were enslaved and lived as foreigners in Egypt until I set you free from your suffering.

In the year of Jubilee, those who are enslaved must be set free to return to their own homes and families. You must not cheat those who are poor and in need, for you yourselves are my servants. Treat others justly, whether they are your own people or strangers in the land."

Wonder & Share ☼

▸ I wonder how we can care for the earth in new ways.
▸ How can we remind ourselves to treat everyone fairly?
▸ Share a freedom story or song.

Pray 💬

Say or sing a joyful prayer of celebration. Make the sound of a trumpet or play an instrument at the beginning and end of your prayer.

Peace Path ⌇
Let It Grow

The people were to let the land rest every seven years. God promised to provide food for the people during that year. I wonder how God did that. How might the land have been different after a year of rest?

☞ **PAGE 70**

Strong Sisters

NUMBERS 27:1-11

DURING THE TIME when the Israelites wandered in the wilderness, there were five sisters named Mahlah, Noah, Hoglah, Milcah, and Tirzah. They had no brothers or husbands, and their father, Zelophehad, had died in the wilderness.

The Israelites approached Canaan, the land God had chosen for them. Moses and the leaders prepared to divide the land among the men of Israel. The sisters had a problem: without their father they would have no right to their own land or homes in Canaan. How would they survive?

The sisters went to Moses, the high priest, the leaders, and the whole congregation of Israel at the Tent of Meeting. Mahlah, Noah, Hoglah, Milcah, and Tirzah stood strong together and said to Moses: "Our father died in the wilderness, leaving no sons. Give us his land. That way our father's name can be remembered through us."

No one had ever brought this kind of request to Moses before. What would he do?

Moses took the sisters' words to the Lord directly. God told Moses, "Mahlah, Noah, Hoglah, Milcah, and Tirzah are honest and righteous in what they are asking. Give them the land belonging to their father."

But this is not where the story ended. God told Moses to change the holy law of Israel so that other women like these sisters would be able to have their father's inheritance if he had no sons.

Wonder & Share 💡

▸ I wonder how each sister felt about talking to Moses.
▸ Which four people would you want beside you in a hard or scary situation?
▸ Learn about women and girls who have helped change unjust laws or rules.

Pray 💬

When Moses did not know what to do, he talked to God. Ask God to help you with a decision in your life.

Peace Path 🕊️
God Welcomes All

How did God care for the five sisters in this story? What does this show about God? Learn more about the five sisters by reading Numbers 26:33; Numbers 36:1–12; Joshua 17:3–6; and 1 Chronicles 7:15.

✍ PAGE 256

The Promised Land

JOSHUA 1:1-9; 3-4

AFTER MOSES DIED, God chose Joshua as the new leader for the Israelites. God said to Joshua, "Lead Israel across the Jordan River into Canaan, the land I promised to give you. I will always be with you and help you as I helped Moses. Be strong and brave! Don't fear. I will be with you wherever you go."

The Jordan River rushed past Joshua, overflowing from the winter rains. How could they possibly cross?

At God's command, Joshua sent leaders throughout the camp to prepare the people. They shouted, "When you see the priests carrying the Ark of the Covenant, it is time to cross the river. Follow them."

The people packed up their tents and bags and got ready to go. The priests stepped into the water with the Ark of the Covenant. Right as their feet touched the water, the river stopped flowing!

The priests stood in the dry riverbed while all the people walked across on dry land.

God told Joshua to send 12 people back to the riverbed and gather 12 rocks, one for each of the 12 tribes of Israel. They brought the rocks to the camp.

The priests left the river. Right away the Jordan River flooded its banks again. This is how God showed the people that Joshua was their leader.

Joshua piled up the 12 rocks to help the people remember what God had done. He said, "Someday your children will ask about the rocks. Tell them God dried up the river, just as God dried up the Red Sea when we left Egypt. By this all the people of the earth will know the great power of God. Worship God always."

Wonder & Share

▶ I wonder how the children felt about walking to the other side of the river. How would you have felt?

▶ Share about a time you felt afraid. What gives you courage?

Pray

Find 12 small stones or blocks. As you add each one to a pile, say something you are grateful for. Let the pile remind you of God's presence with you.

Peace Path

Water Wonders

After leaving Egypt, the Israelites crossed the Red Sea. In this story, they crossed the Jordan River. Look back at page 58. How are these two events similar and different?

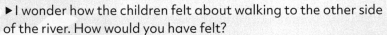 **PAGE 190**

Ruth and Naomi

RUTH 1–4

WHEN JUDGES RULED in Israel there was a great famine. The people could not grow enough food to feed themselves or their animals. So an Israelite woman named Naomi moved to Moab with her husband, Elimelech, and their two sons. Moab was a land with different people, traditions, and beliefs than Israel.

After they moved, Elimelech died, leaving Naomi to raise her sons as a single mother. When the sons grew up, they married women from Moab—Ruth and Orpah. Ten years later, both sons died, leaving no children.

Naomi decided to go back to Bethlehem in Israel. She said to Ruth and Orpah, "Return to your mother's homes. May the Lord give you the same loving-kindness you have given me and my sons."

Orpah and Ruth cried to Naomi, "No, we will go live with you and your people."

Again, Naomi told them to go back to their homes in Moab. "Daughters, I have nothing left to give you. My sons are dead, and I have no way to provide for you. Surely the Lord has turned against me." All three wept together, and Orpah kissed Naomi goodbye.

But Ruth refused to leave. She said to Naomi,

"Do not force me to leave you.
　　Where you go, I will go.
Where you stay, I will stay.
　　Your people will be my people.
Your God will be my God.
　　Where you die, I will die."

Naomi saw that Ruth was determined to go with her, so she agreed. They walked together to Bethlehem.

Naomi and Ruth arrived in Bethlehem at the beginning of the barley harvest. They had no money or land of their own. So Ruth went to glean in the barley field belonging to Boaz, a relative of Naomi's husband. Ruth worked hard all day to gather enough grain. Boaz noticed Ruth and asked his workers, "Who is this woman?" The workers said, "She is from Moab and came here with Naomi."

Boaz spoke to Ruth, "Stay here and work in my field. I will make sure no one bothers you. Drink from my water jars when you are thirsty." Ruth bowed down and said, "Why have you shown me such favor? I am a foreigner from Moab."

Boaz told her, "I have heard of the loving-kindness you showed your mother-in-law Naomi. You came to a foreign land to be with her when you did not have to do so. May our God shelter you as a bird shelters her young under her wings."

Ruth told Naomi what happened. Naomi said, "Blessed be the Lord, whose loving-kindness remembers the living and the dead." Ruth continued to work in Boaz's fields, and she and Naomi had plenty to eat.

At the end of the harvest season, Ruth and Boaz were married. God blessed them with a son named Obed. Many years later, Ruth became the great-grandmother to King David.

Wonder & Share

▶ I wonder how life in Moab was different than in Israel. Find these places on the map on page 363.
▶ Naomi's husband and sons died. Talk about a time something sad happened to you.
▶ Share an example of someone showing loving-kindness to a stranger or outsider.

Pray 💬

Read the first paragraph of Psalm 91 on page 148 as your prayer. What is God compared to in both the story of Ruth and in the psalm?

Peace Path
Let It Grow

God told the Israelites to make sure that women, foreigners, and widows were cared for. Workers were to leave some grain in the fields for them to glean, which means they could gather the food without needing to pay for it.

☞ **PAGE 150**

Hannah's Prayer

1 SAMUEL 1:1–2:11

HANNAH HAD NO CHILDREN with her husband, Elkanah. Elkanah loved Hannah very much, even though she couldn't bear children. Elkanah's other wife, Peninnah, had many children, and she mocked Hannah for years. Hannah was heartbroken; she wept and did not eat.

Hannah decided to go to God's house. She was so upset that she cried while she prayed. "God of hosts," Hannah promised, "if you remember me and give me a child, I will dedicate my child to you." Hannah continued praying silently.

Eli the priest saw Hannah's lips moving but could not hear her words. He thought she was drunk. "How long will you do this?" he asked. "Put away your wine."

"I am not drunk," Hannah asserted. "I am deeply sad. I am pouring my heart out to God."

Eli said, "Go in peace. May God give you what you desire."

When Hannah went home, she felt like eating and drinking again. She no longer looked so sad. God remembered her, and in time, she became pregnant. Hannah had a son! She named him Samuel, which means, "God has heard."

Hannah kept her promise to God. Once Samuel was old enough, she took him to God's house. She prayed:

"My heart sings praises to God.
   I am strong in God. I rejoice in my victory.
No one else is holy like God.
   No one is a rock like our God.
God brings death but also life.
   God lifts the poor from the dust.
God honors those who don't have what they need.
God will guard the faithful
   and give strength to the anointed one."

Hannah traveled home, and Samuel remained to live in God's house. Each year Hannah made a new robe for Samuel and brought it to him.

Wonder & Share

▶ Having a child was so important to Hannah. I wonder what important things you want God to do for you.

▶ Share about a time you felt sad and a time you felt strong.

Pray

Which lines of Hannah's prayer (in bold) do you like best? Which line do you think is most important? Say a prayer that uses some or all of Hannah's words.

Art Spotlight

The illustrator drew Hannah wearing a Mexican shawl called a *rebozo*. The *nopal* (prickly pear cactus) represents hope and endurance. The flower that grows on the cactus represents the love of a mother.

Here I Am

1 SAMUEL 3

AFTER HANNAH brought her son Samuel to the temple, he served God with Eli the priest. Samuel slept in the room where the Ark of the Covenant was kept. The lamp of God burned brightly. One night Samuel was awakened by a voice calling, "Samuel, Samuel."

Samuel went to Eli and said, "Here I am." But Eli had not called him. So Samuel went back to bed.

Again God called to him, "Samuel, Samuel."

Samuel went back to Eli and said, "Here I am." But Eli had not called him. So Samuel went back to bed.

This happened a third time! Samuel went to Eli and said, "Here I am."

Eli told Samuel, "I am not calling you. God is calling you! Next time you hear the voice, say, 'I am listening, God. What do you want me to do?'"

Samuel heard the voice again. This time he said, "I am listening, God. What do you want me to do?"

God said, "Eli knew that his sons scorned me and yet did nothing to stop them. I warned Eli, but he did not listen. Punishment is about to come to Eli's family."

Samuel lay awake until morning. He was afraid to tell Eli what God had said.

The next morning Eli said, "Samuel, my son. What did God tell you? Don't hide anything from me." So Samuel bravely told him everything.

Eli knew that he and his sons had done wrong. He replied, "God will do what is right."

As Samuel grew, God was with him. Soon everyone knew that Samuel was truly God's prophet. God appeared to him often and told him what to say.

Wonder & Share

▸ I wonder how God's voice sounded.
▸ Share a story of someone who spoke up and told the truth even when it was hard.

Pray

Say a prayer before bed. Take time to both speak and listen for God's voice.

Art Spotlight

The Mexican sunflowers in this scene symbolize loyalty and faith. Where do you see these qualities in Samuel and Eli?

David the Shepherd

1 SAMUEL 16:1-13

WHEN SAMUEL THE PROPHET GREW OLD, the leaders of Israel came to him and said, "Give us a king to rule over us, just like all the other nations." Samuel anointed Saul as the king. King Saul failed to obey God, so a time came when God wanted Samuel to choose a different king.

God said to him, "Go to the home of Jesse in Bethlehem. One of his sons will be the next king."

Samuel went to Jesse's home. Jesse's oldest son, Eliab, came to Samuel. He was tall and good looking. "Eliab must be the new king," thought Samuel. But God said, "Do not look at his appearance or his height. That is not what I am concerned about. I look at a person's heart. Eliab is not the one."

Next came Abinadab and Shammah. God had not chosen them to be king either. Four more sons came, but they were not the ones.

Samuel said to Jesse, "Are all your sons here?"

Jesse replied, "No. My youngest son, David, is in the field taking care of the sheep."

"Send for him," said Samuel.

When David came, God said to Samuel, "Pour oil on David's head as a sign that someday he will be my chosen king."

Samuel poured oil on David's head while his family watched. God's Spirit was on David from that day forward.

Wonder & Share

▶ I wonder how David felt when Samuel anointed him. What do you think his brothers said to him later?
▶ Share about a time you were left out and a time you were chosen.

Pray

David wrote many psalms. Read Psalm 23 on page 86 as your prayer.

Practice Peace

Do you ever compare your clothing or hair or the shape of your body to others? It's easy to judge ourselves and others by how we look. However, God told Samuel that what *truly* matters is what's inside. Name some inner qualities you have, such as patience, courage, or kindness.

Abigail's Idea
1 SAMUEL 25:1-35

ABIGAIL LIVED IN CARMEL with her husband, Nabal. Abigail was wise and beautiful, but Nabal was mean.

Nabal and Abigail were rich and owned thousands of goats and sheep. Sheep shearing season had arrived, and it was time for Nabal's shepherds to cut off the sheep's wool.

David and his men were living in the nearby wilderness. David's men knew Nabal's shepherds and kept them safe. David sent a greeting to Nabal. "Peace to you and your household," David's messenger said. "We've helped your shepherds in the past. Will you share food and drink with us now?"

Usually, the people of Israel gave food and drink to those who asked. But Nabal replied, "Who is David? Why should I offer him food and drink?"

Nabal had plenty, but he still did not want to share. Nabal's response angered David. "Strap on your swords!" David commanded his men. He planned to fight Nabal's whole household.

When Abigail discovered David's plan, she quickly gathered bread, wine, grain, meat, raisins, and fig cakes. She loaded everything on donkeys and sent her servants to bring it to David. She did not tell Nabal.

Abigail followed her servants and met David and his men. She got off her donkey and bowed before David, saying, "Don't take foolish Nabal's words to heart. Please accept my gift, forgive Nabal, and do not kill innocent people. The Lord will keep you safe from your enemies, and you will be king. When you are king, remember me."

"Blessed be the Lord!" David said. "God sent you to me today. Blessed be your wisdom and blessed are you for showing me I should not kill or seek revenge. I will not hurt you." David accepted her gift and went away in peace.

Wonder & Share

▶ Imagine that Nabal *did* share with David. What might have happened next?

▶ Share examples of gifts you have given and gifts you have received.

Pray 💬

Pray for peace in your family, your community, your country, and the world. Look at a world map to discover countries to pray for.

Peace Path
Love Your Enemies

What did Abigail do to bring peace? Look at the "Peace with Others" ideas on pages 352–353. When have you used one of those peace ideas?

PAGE 108

King David's Table

2 SAMUEL 5:1–5; 8:15–9:13

WHEN DAVID WAS A BOY, the prophet Samuel had anointed him as the future king. When he was 30 years old, the leaders of Israel came together and said to him, "In the past, Saul was our king. But God chose you to be a shepherd and ruler for us." They anointed David and he served as king over Israel for 40 years. He treated people with fairness and justice.

One day King David asked his servant, "Is there anyone from King Saul's family who is still alive? His son Jonathan was my friend, and I want to do something kind for his family."

Ziba, a servant from the house of Saul, was called. He said, "Jonathan's son Mephibosheth is still alive. When he was five years old, both of his feet were badly injured. Even now as an adult, he cannot walk."

David sent for him. Mephibosheth threw himself on his face in front of David.

David said, "Don't be afraid. Your father and I were close friends, so I will be kind to you. I will give you your grandfather Saul's land. You will eat at my table from now on."

Mephibosheth said, "Why do you care about me? I'm no good. I'm nothing but a dead dog."

But David did care. He called for Ziba and said, "I am giving Saul's land back to Mephibosheth. Work the land for him and bring in the crops so that his family and servants will have food. As for Mephibosheth, he will always eat with me."

From then on, Mephibosheth came to live in Jerusalem. He ate at David's table, just like one of David's sons. And Mephibosheth had a young son of his own named Mica.

Wonder & Share

▶ I wonder how Mephibosheth felt at the beginning, middle, and end of the story.

▶ Share about a time you felt like you weren't good enough. Then read the speech bubbles on page 351 aloud.

Pray 💬

David and Mephibosheth ate meals together. As part of your mealtime prayer, thank God for the person sitting next to you.

Peace Path 🏃
Love Your Neighbor

David did not just *talk* about caring about Mephibosheth. He took action! What things did David do? How can you show love to your neighbors?

✍️ **PAGE 200**

Parable for a King

2 SAMUEL 11:1–12:15

KING DAVID FOLLOWED GOD'S WAYS, but he still sometimes made choices that displeased God. When David fell in love with Bathsheba, she was already married. David arranged for her husband to be killed, and then he took Bathsheba as his own wife.

God sent the prophet Nathan to confront David about these choices. Nathan told David this story:

"There were two men. One was rich, the other was poor. The rich man owned many flocks of sheep. The poor man only had one little lamb. The lamb grew up with the man and his children. The poor man shared his food with the lamb, and even let the lamb drink from his cup. He held the lamb close to his chest. It was like the lamb was part of the family. A traveler came to the rich man. Since the Israelites usually offered food and drink to their guests, the rich man wanted to prepare a meal for the traveler. But the rich man did not want to use one of his own sheep for food, so he took the poor man's lamb to use for food instead."

David's anger flashed. "How could the rich man do this? He deserves to be punished! He should give the poor man back four more lambs because he had no pity," David said.

"You are like this man!" Nathan said. "God made you king of Israel. God rescued you from danger and gave you a home and a family. If you wanted more, God would have given you much more. But you killed Bathsheba's husband, took her as your wife, and kept it a secret. There will be consequences."

"I hurt God and others, and what I did was wrong!" David confessed.

"God forgives you," Nathan said, "but that does not change the harm you caused. Terrible things will happen because of what you have done."

Wonder & Share

▶ I wonder how the poor man felt when the rich man took his lamb.

▶ Nathan confronted David's wrongdoing with a story. What stories have helped you learn?

Pray

Use your finger to slowly follow the prayer path on page 347. As you move toward the middle, tell God something you did wrong. Then return to the outside, imagining God's love and forgiveness surrounding you.

Dig In

Nathan was the court prophet for King David, so this was not the first time Nathan spoke to him. In 2 Samuel 7, God came to Nathan in a vision and told him about the covenant between God and David. Nathan also wrote a history of David's life.

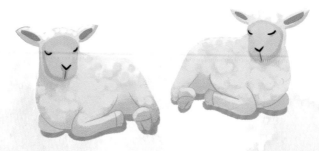

Song of a Shepherd

PSALM 23

A Psalm of David

THE LORD is my shepherd,
    I will not be in need.
The shepherd brings me to green fields,
    and leads me by quiet waters.
The shepherd gives life to my soul,
    and leads me in the right paths.

Even when I go through the darkest valley,
    I am not afraid.
For the shepherd is with me,
    with a rod and staff to protect me.

The Lord prepares a feast for me
    as my enemies watch nearby.
The Lord anoints my head with oil.
My cup overflows.
    Goodness and love will follow me,
every day of my life.
    I will live in the Lord's house all my days.

Wonder & Share

▸ I wonder how God leads us.
▸ Share about a hard or painful time in your life. How did you feel? Who helped you?

Pray

Express your prayer through art. Draw green fields, water, and a valley. In the fields and water, draw things that make you feel happy and peaceful. In the valley, draw things that worry or upset you. Finish by saying "Amen!"

Peace Path

I Am Not Alone

How do you feel when you read this psalm? What is comforting about these words of David? David knew that God is always with us—in the happy, peaceful events of our lives and in the most difficult experiences we have.

PAGE 112

Song of Wonder

PSALM 139

A Psalm of David

O LORD, you search me and know me.
    You know when I sit and when I rise.
You know my thoughts,
    and each path I take.
Even before I speak, you know my words.
    You protect me behind and in front.
This is such wonderful news!
    It is hard to believe!

Where can I go from you? Where could I hide?
    If I go to heaven, you are there.
If I go to the farthest ocean, you are there.
    Your hand will safely lead me.
I might say, "The darkness will cover me,
    the light will become night."
But for you, the night is as bright as the day.

You formed me inside and out.
    You knit me together in my mother's womb.
I praise you, for I am made in a wonderful way.
    You knew all about me,
even when I was being made in secret.
    In your book you wrote all the days of my life.
Your thoughts are amazing, God.
    I could try to count them,
but they are more than the sand on the seashore.

Search me, O God, and know my heart.
    Test me and know my every thought.
See if there is any hurtful way inside me,
    and lead me in the way everlasting.

Wonder & Share

▶ I wonder what will happen in your life as you get older. Imagine God with you at every age.
▶ Read aloud one or two lines from the psalm that bring you joy or comfort.

Pray

For God, the night is as bright as the day. Pray a morning prayer and an evening prayer from page 342.

Peace Path

I Am Special

Imagine God forming your body. You were made in a wonderful way! Thank God for your body.

PAGE 118

King Solomon

1 KINGS 3–11

KING SOLOMON loved and followed God, just like his father, King David, had. One night, God appeared to Solomon in a dream.

"Ask for what I should give you," God said.

"You showed my father, King David, great love," Solomon replied. "And now, even though I am only a child, you have made me king in his place. Yet, I do not know how to be a good king for so many people. Will you give me wisdom?"

God felt pleased that Solomon asked for wisdom.

"Since you asked for an understanding heart instead of a long life or riches for yourself, I will do what you ask," God said. "I will give you a strong mind, and there will be no one like you. I will also give you riches and honor. Continue to listen to my important words, and I will give you a long life."

Solomon woke up from his dream. He went to Jerusalem, where he burned offerings to God and made a feast for those who served him.

The people of Israel were so numerous, it was like trying to count sand on the seashore. They had plenty to eat and drink. The people were happy and lived in peace and safety while Solomon was their king.

Solomon's vast heart was the wisest in all the land. He wrote thousands of songs and proverbs. He knew about different trees, plants, birds, fish, reptiles, and other animals. People flocked from all over the earth to hear his wisdom.

Four hundred eighty years after God freed the Israelites from slavery in Egypt, King Solomon enslaved people to build a holy temple for God. The temple had great rooms, many windows, and three levels. The walls and doors had engravings of angels, trees, and flowers. Everything was covered with gold.

When the enslaved workers finished building God's house, King Solomon brought all the elders and leaders of Israel to Jerusalem. The priests carried the Ark of the Covenant. The ark held Moses' two stone tablets, a reminder of God's covenant. The priests placed the ark inside the most holy sanctuary of the temple. God's splendor filled the house like a cloud.

Then Solomon stood in front of the altar, lifted his hands to the sky, and prayed:

"God, there is no one that loves like you in heaven or on earth. You keep your promises to those who follow you with an open heart. Your covenant and love never end. But will you stay here in this place? Nothing can hold you. How can this house I built contain you? But please listen to my prayers and the prayers of your people and keep your name in this place."

After the temple was finished, God spoke to Solomon again, saying, "My name and my heart will always remain in the house you built for me, as long as you continue to walk with me. If you or your children forget me and worship other gods, the people of Israel will no longer live in peace. They will leave the land I gave them. And this house you built for me will be ruined."

Time passed and King Solomon grew richer than anyone else on earth. He enslaved people from foreign lands to build a palace for himself. The laborers built him a throne of ivory and pure gold. The magnificent and witty Queen of Sheba even came to visit him. But King Solomon was losing sight of God's important words about how to live. He married hundreds of women. He worshiped other gods and built altars to them.

God said to Solomon, "You have stopped following my ways. I will take this kingdom from you and give it to someone else."

Enemies of Israel began to make trouble for Solomon in the last days of his reign, but God honored the covenant God made with the people of Israel.

Wonder & Share

▶ If God came to you in a dream, what would you ask God to give you?

▶ I wonder how God felt about King Solomon using enslaved people to build God's house. See a diagram and learn more about Solomon's temple on page 366.

▶ Israel lived in peace when Solomon was king. Name or learn about wise people who help make peace.

Pray

Ask God to give you wisdom, like Solomon did. Imagine the cloud of God's glory surrounding you as you pray.

Live It

Turn to page 97 and read some of the wise sayings that Solomon wrote, called proverbs. Which one do you like best? Write your own wise saying.

Solomon's Wise Sayings

SELECTIONS FROM PROVERBS (CEV)

King Solomon wrote thousands of wise sayings called proverbs:

11:13
A gossip tells everything,
but a true friend
will keep a secret.

11:17
Kindness is rewarded—
but if you are cruel,
you hurt yourself.

11:27
Try hard to do right,
and you will win friends;
go looking for trouble,
and you will find it.

12:25
Worry is a heavy burden,
but a kind word
always brings cheer.

14:10
No one else can really know
how sad or happy you are.

15:1
A kind answer
soothes angry feelings,
but harsh words
stir them up.

15:17
A simple meal with love
is better than a feast
where there is hatred.

16:24
Kind words are like honey—
they cheer you up
and make you feel strong.

20:27
Our inner thoughts
are a lamp
from the Lord,
and they search our hearts.

24:14
Wisdom is like honey
for your life—
if you find it,
your future is bright.

24:26
Giving an honest answer
is a sign
of true friendship.

25:11
The right word
at the right time
is like precious gold
set in silver.

25:21
If your enemies are hungry,
give them something to eat.
And if they are thirsty,
give them something
to drink.

Wonder & Share

▶ Share your ideas for being a true friend.
▶ What kind things could you say to cheer someone up this week?

Pray 💬

Solomon said that worry is a heavy burden. What are you worried about today? Tell God your worries. Then imagine God carrying them for you.

Dig In 📖

Read Proverbs 25:21 on this page. Jesus gives a similar message in the parable on page 248. These words are also repeated in Romans 12:20 by the apostle Paul in his letter to the church in Rome.

A Love Song

SONG OF SONGS

I AM BLACK, and I am beautiful.
    I am like a rose or a lily of the valley.
My beloved is like an apple tree,
    with satisfying and sweet fruit.

Let my beloved kiss me. For love is better than wine.
    I adore my beloved's name. It is like perfume.

The one I love comes to me as swiftly
    as a young deer, bounding up a mountain.
"Come away with me, beautiful one," my beloved calls.
    "Winter is over. Flowers bloom. Figs hang from the fig trees.
Spring is here! Let me see your face and hear your voice.
    For your voice is tender and your face is lovely.
Shall we catch the little foxes that ruin our blossoming vineyards?"

My beloved is mine, and I am my beloved's.

"How beautiful you are, my darling," my beloved says.
    "Behind your veil, your eyes are like doves. Your hair
and mouth are delightful. Your cheeks
    are like pomegranates. You are flawless.
You have stolen my heart with the goodness
    of your love. You are like a garden with an orchard,
fragrant spices, and a well of living water."

My beloved is radiant, with curls as black
    as a raven's feathers, arms like gold, and legs
like alabaster. My beloved appears
    precious to me, like gems or cedar trees from Lebanon.
I love hearing my beloved speak sweetly to me.

I am my beloved's, and my beloved is mine.

Love is as strong as death,
    as powerful as a fire's flame.
No flood can drown love.

Wonder & Share 💡

▶ God made all the shades of our skin beautiful. I wonder how we can celebrate God's beauty in ourselves and in each other.

▶ What makes you feel loved?

Pray 💬

Sing or listen to a song that expresses love for God. Try writing new words to the tune of one of your favorite songs!

Live It ☀

Tell someone how much you love them and why. What makes that person special?

One More Meal

1 KINGS 17:1-16

AFTER KING SOLOMON DIED, the Israelites split into two kingdoms: the northern kingdom of Israel, and the southern kingdom of Judah.

Ahab was the seventh king of the northern kingdom of Israel. He did not follow God's ways. He and his wife Jezebel built a temple and altar to the god Baal. God sent the prophet Elijah to warn King Ahab that there would be no rain for three years because he had turned away from the one true God.

Then God said to Elijah, "Go hide by the Cherith Creek, east of the Jordan River. Drink the water from the creek. I will bring food for you."

So Elijah went. Two times every day, ravens brought bread and meat to him. But there was no rain, and soon the creek dried up. Elijah did not have anything to drink.

God said, "Go to Zarephath. A widow in that town will give you water and food."

When Elijah came to Zarephath, he saw a widow picking up sticks for her fire. He said, "Can I have a cup of water?" She went to get it. He said, "Can I also have a piece of bread?"

The widow replied, "I do not have any bread. I only have a bit of flour and oil. I got these sticks so I can make one more fire and cook one last meal for my son and me."

Elijah said, "Do not worry! Go home and make food for you and your son. But first make me a small piece of bread. God promises that your flour and oil will not run out before there is rain for the crops!"

The widow did what Elijah said. And every day there was enough flour and oil to make more food.

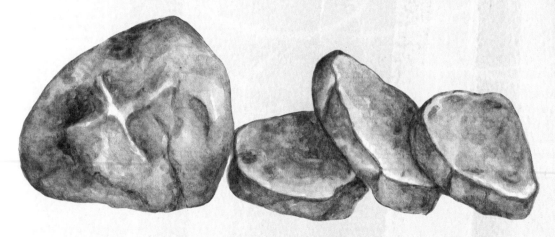

Wonder & Share 💡

▸ Imagine a jar of oil that never runs out.
▸ When have you shared with someone? How does it feel when someone shares with you?

Pray 💬

Pray the third meal prayer from page 344.

Dig In 📖

King Ahab and Queen Jezebel lived in Samaria, the capital city of Israel. Learn more about the kingdoms of Israel and Judah on pages 364–365. The maps show how the land was divided.

A Generous Woman

2 KINGS 4:8-37

GOD TOLD ELIJAH to anoint Elisha as a prophet to serve Israel after him. The two traveled and worked together. After Elijah was taken to heaven in a whirlwind, Elisha received his power as a prophet of God.

Elisha often traveled near the town of Shunem. A rich woman lived there with her family. She knew Elisha was a holy man of God. So she made a room for him on the roof of her house. She put a bed, table, chair, and oil lamp in it. When Elisha came to town, he always stayed there.

Elisha was grateful for her kindness and generosity. How could he thank her? Elisha's servant Gehazi had an idea: "Her husband is old, and she does not have a son."

Elisha went to the woman and said, "Next year, you will have a baby."

"Please don't lie to me!" the woman said. She did not believe this could happen, but it came to pass. She gave birth to a son.

One day, her son was out in the field with his father. The son said, "My head hurts!" A servant carried the boy to his mother. She held him all morning, but then he died. She laid him on the bed in Elisha's room, saddled her donkey, and hurried across the plains to Mount Carmel where Elisha was.

The woman fell down at Elisha's feet and told him the terrible news. Elisha went back to the house with her. He lay close to the boy and prayed. The boy sneezed seven times and opened his eyes!

The woman was overjoyed that her son was alive again. She bowed down at Elisha's feet in gratitude. Then she held her son close.

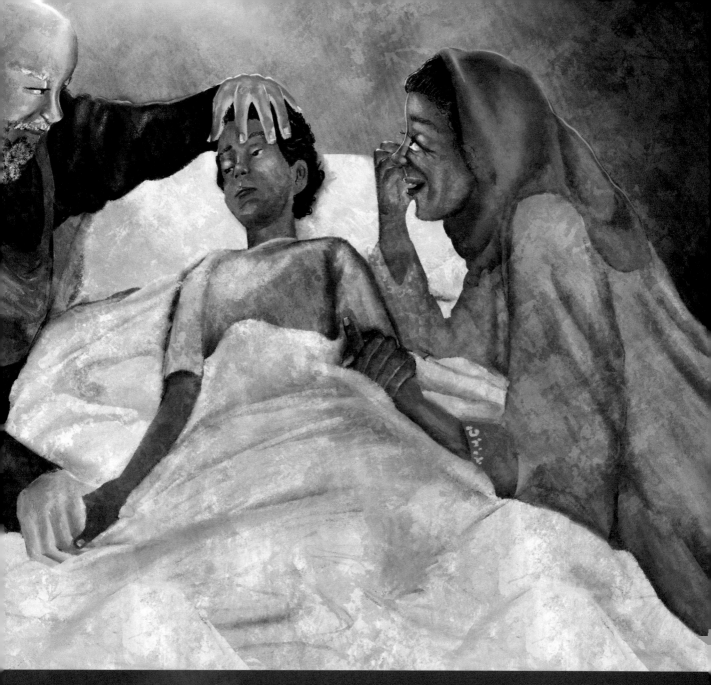

Wonder & Share

▸ I wonder how the woman knew Elisha was a holy man of God.

▸ How can you make your home a welcoming place for visitors?

▸ Share about a time someone was kind to you. How did you show your thanks?

Pray 💬

The woman's son became very sick. Pray for people you know who are feeling sick or pray for people in a nearby hospital.

Dig In 📖

In biblical times, many houses had flat roofs that formed an open-air room for visiting, hanging laundry, praying, or sleeping. Have you ever slept outside?

King Josiah

2 KINGS 22:1–23:25

KING AMON OF JUDAH did many evil things and was killed by the people of Judah. They made his son Josiah king when Josiah was just eight years old. Josiah's mother, Jedidah, taught him to follow God's ways. Josiah did what was right, just like King David had.

After ruling for 18 years, King Josiah hired carpenters, masons, and builders to fix God's temple in Jerusalem. While they worked on the temple, the high priest Hilkiah discovered a lost book of God's laws.

Hilkiah sent his secretary, Shaphan, to King Josiah. Shaphan read the book aloud to the king. As Josiah listened, he felt so upset he cried and tore his clothes. Josiah worried God might be angry. None of the people of Judah were living by the important words God gave them in the book.

Josiah sent Hilkiah and Shaphan to speak to Huldah the prophetess. God gave her a message for Josiah. Huldah said, "This is what God says: my people should not have forgotten me or worshiped other gods. But because you are so sorry, you will die in peace."

King Josiah brought all the people together to God's temple. He read God's book to them and reminded the people of God's holy covenant with them. Together they promised to follow God's ways. At Passover time, Josiah said, "Remember that God freed you from slavery in Egypt. We must celebrate Passover the way God has commanded in the book Hilkiah found."

Josiah honored God by following the words in God's book. He destroyed all the idols and altars to other gods in the land of Judah. Josiah was a special king because he loved God with all the strength of his heart and soul. There was no other king like him.

Wonder & Share ☀

▶ I wonder how Josiah's mother, Jedidah, helped him learn to follow God.
▶ Whom do you love with all your heart?

Pray 💬

Josiah hired people to rebuild the temple. Pray a building prayer. Stack blocks as you name people and situations you want to pray for today.

Dig In 📖

Josiah was king of Judah for 31 years, from about 640–609 BCE. The book that the priest found in the temple was most likely Deuteronomy, the fourth book of the Old Testament. You can read verses from Deuteronomy at the bottom of page 62.

Rebellion and Ruin

2 KINGS 24:18-25:15

AFTER KING JOSIAH'S DEATH, three of his sons and his nephew served as kings of Judah. His third son, Zedekiah, became king when he was 21 years old and ruled for 11 years. He did many evil things, just as his older brother and grandfather had done.

At that time, Judah was being ruled by the nation of Babylon. Zedekiah hated this and so he rebelled against King Nebuchadnezzar of Babylon. The army of Babylon marched to Jerusalem. For eighteen months, the army camped around the city. No one could go in or out. By that time, there was no food left inside the city.

Finally, the Babylonian army broke through the city wall. In the dark of night, King Zedekiah and his soldiers tried to escape. They sneaked through a back gate, past the king's garden, and out into the plains. But the Babylonian army chased them and caught Zedekiah, bringing him back to King Nebuchadnezzar to be punished. He was put in chains and taken to Babylon.

The Babylonians destroyed the temple and took away all the valuable things made from gold, silver, and bronze. The army burned the royal palace and all the houses and important buildings in Jerusalem. They tore down the walls around the city. They forced most of the people to go faraway to Babylon as prisoners. Only a few farmers who had very little money were left behind to work in the fields and vineyards.

Wonder & Share

▶ I wonder how the people of Jerusalem helped each other during this terrible time.
▶ Share your feelings about this story. What makes you feel sad, angry, or scared?

Pray

There are many people who are currently experiencing war or other types of violence. Pray for peace and safety in your community and around the world.

Dig In

This story begins what is known as the Babylonian exile. Find the exile on the Old Testament timeline on pages 358–359. See how many years it was before the people of Judah went back to Jerusalem.

Swords and Plows

ISAIAH 2:1-5

DURING A TIME of war and sadness, God gave Isaiah the prophet a vision of peace:

In the coming days,
   the mountain of God's house
will be the highest of all mountains.
   It will be raised above every hill.
All nations will stream to it.
   Many people will say,
"Let us go up to the mountain of God,
   to the house of the God of Jacob.
We want God to teach us.
   We want to walk in God's path."
God will teach the people,
   and help them live in peace.
There will be no more fighting or war.
   Nations will turn their swords into plows,
and their spears into garden tools.
   Nations will not raise their swords
or learn the ways of war anymore.
   Come, let us live in the light of God!

Wonder & Share

▸ Imagine all people on earth going up a mountain to God's house together.

▸ I wonder how we can live in the light of God.

▸ How are weapons used as tools in the picture? Share a creative idea for turning a weapon into a tool for peace.

Pray

Look at a map. Choose pairs of countries that are next to each other. Pray that they will live together peacefully. Now choose pairs of countries that are far away from each other. Conflicts can still happen from a distance! Pray for peace between those countries.

Peace Path

Love Your Enemies

Sometimes friends, family members, or neighbors disagree or get in fights. But sometimes whole nations fight against each other with armies. We wait with hope for the day when nations stop going to war!

PAGE 206

A New King

ISAIAH 11:1–9

AFTER JERUSALEM WAS DESTROYED and the people of Judah were forced to go to Babylon, God gave them a message of hope through the prophet Isaiah:

Like a branch that sprouts from a stump,
    a king will be born from the family of David.
God's Spirit will rest on him—
    the spirit of wisdom,
    the spirit of strength,
    the spirit of understanding.
The king will find great joy
    in following the ways of the Lord.

The king will not judge people by how they look,
    or be swayed by what others say about them.
Instead, he will treat the poor fairly,
    and will make wise decisions for those who suffer.
Righteousness and justice will be his belt.
    faithfulness will surround him.

The wolf will live with the lamb.
    The leopard will lie down with the goat.
The calf and lion will be together,
    and a little child will lead them.
Cows and bears will eat together.
    Calves and cubs will rest together.
Babies and young children will play near snakes
    and be safe.
No one will be hurt on God's holy mountain.
    Just as water fills the sea,
the whole earth will be full of
    people who know and love the Lord.

Wonder & Share

▶ I wonder who the king is that Isaiah spoke about.
▶ I wonder how we can care for people who suffer.
▶ What animals would you like to play with?

Pray

Ask the Spirit of God to be with you, giving you wisdom, strength, and understanding.

Peace Path

God's Spirit Moves

What did you notice about God's Spirit in Isaiah's message? How will God's Spirit help the coming king?

PAGE 120

Lift the Valleys

ISAIAH 40:1–11

MANY YEARS PASSED. Would the people of
Judah ever be able to return home from exile in
Babylon? God gave them another message through
the prophet Isaiah:

Comfort, comfort my people,
    says your God.
This hard time will end!

A voice says,
"Prepare the way of the Lord!
    Make a straight road in the desert for our God.
The valleys will be lifted up.
    The mountains and hills will be made low.
The crooked will be straight,
    the rough places will be smooth.
Then all people will see God's glory."

People are like grass.
    Grass grows and then it dies.
But God's words last forever.

I have good news for you!
    Shout it from the mountaintop!
With a strong voice cry out,
    "Here is your God!"
God comes with power
    to make all things right.

God will feed the flock like a shepherd,
    God will gather up the lambs,
and gently carry them.
    God will lead the mother sheep.

Wonder & Share 💡

▶ I wonder how we can prepare the way of the Lord.
▶ The children in the picture are lifting the valleys! How could you and your friends work together to make a more peaceful world?

Pray 💬

Isaiah said, "I have good news for you!" Share good news with God in prayer.

Peace Path

I Am Not Alone

What worries or concerns do you have? No matter what is happening around you, God is always there. Imagine God caring for you like a shepherd cares for a mother sheep and her lambs.

Fly like an Eagle

ISAIAH 40:12-31

AS THE YEARS OF EXILE in Babylon went on, the people of Judah began to wonder if God cared about them anymore. God sent the prophet Isaiah with another message:

"Did you create the sky and the ocean?
Did you fill a bucket with the dirt of the earth?
Did you weigh the hills?
Are you God's teacher? Do you help God understand things?
Next to God, the nations and land are like dust and sand.
Who compares with God?
Is God a fancy idol made of bronze or special wood?

Don't you know? Haven't you heard?
Hasn't someone told you?
God made the earth and rules over it.
Next to God, we are like tiny insects.
God brings down rulers.
They are like flowers that grow for a while,
but then are carried off in a storm.
Look at the sky.
Who made the stars? Who gave them names?
God is so strong that even the stars cannot be lost.

Sometimes you say, 'God is not watching.
God doesn't care if bad things happen to us.'
How can you say that?
Don't you know? Haven't you heard?
Hasn't someone told you?
God is the great Creator and knows all things.
Look to God when you feel tired.
Wait for the Lord and receive strength.
You will be like an eagle in the sky.
You will run without getting tired.
You will walk and not faint!"

Wonder & Share

▶ I wonder why the people thought that God did not care about them anymore.

▶ When have you felt tired and in need of strength? How can you care for your body when you feel that way?

Pray 💬

Isaiah names many things from nature. Go outside or look out a window as you pray for creation. Look at the "Peace with Creation" ideas on pages 354–355 for ways to help care for the earth.

Peace Path
I Need Comfort

Have you ever felt like God wasn't watching or helping you? Isaiah reminded people that God knows all things, including what you are going through. Look to God when you feel alone, sad, or discouraged.

👈 **PAGE 148**

Wolves and Lambs

ISAIAH 65:17-25

GOD HAD PROMISED to bring the people of Judah back to their homeland. But what would it be like? When they last saw Jerusalem, all the buildings, the temple, and the palace were burning. The walls were being torn down. Even if they made it back home, where would they live and worship?

Again, God spoke to the people through the prophet Isaiah and said,

> "I am making a new heaven and a new earth.
>   No one will remember the painful things from the past.
> My people will live in Jerusalem again.
>   They will live long and happy lives.
> No longer will there be weeping or distress.
>   The city will be filled with joy.
> Babies and children will be healthy,
>   Old people will feel young.
> My people will build their own houses
>   and grow their own grapes.
> They will live to be as old as trees!
>   I will answer their prayers before they even speak.
> Wolves and lambs will eat together.
>   Lions will eat straw like the oxen do.
> The serpent will eat dust.
>   The animals will not hurt each other anymore."

Wonder & Share

▶ I wonder how God makes the earth new.
▶ How do you like to celebrate? When something great happens, whom do you tell first?

Pray 💬

Isaiah talks about people of all ages. Pray for a baby, toddler, school-aged child, teenager, young adult, middle-aged person, and an older adult.

Peace Path

Nature Trail

Draw a picture of the parts of creation that Isaiah names in this prophecy. Learn something about each one. For instance, did you know that trees can live for thousands of years?

☞ PAGE 140

Written on Your Heart

JEREMIAH 29, 31

THE NORTHERN KINGDOM OF ISRAEL and the southern kingdom of Judah had split apart many years before. The people of Judah were exiles in Babylon, far from their home. The prophet Jeremiah sent a letter to them with this message from God: "I know the plans I have for you. They are plans for goodness and not for harm, to give you a future with hope. When you call for me in prayer, I will hear you. When you search for me, you will find me, if you seek me with all your heart. I will gather you from faraway lands. I will bring you back to your home."

Then God gave Jeremiah a message for the people of Israel:

"I have loved you with an everlasting love,
    I am always faithful to you.
Once again you will play your tambourines,
    and dance with great joy.
You will plant vineyards on the mountains of Samaria,
    and enjoy a great harvest of fruit.
Sing for joy for the people of Judah!
    See, I am going to bring them from the
farthest parts of the earth.
    I will gather those who cannot see or walk,
the pregnant and birthing mothers,
    all my people who will return.
I, the Lord who scattered Judah, will gather them
    like a shepherd gathers a flock.
I will lead them to streams of water,
    on a straight path where they will not stumble.
I will turn their sadness into joy,
    I will comfort them and give them
gladness instead of grief."

"Soon I will make a new covenant with both Israel and Judah. I will put my law within them and write it on their hearts. I will be their God, and they will be my people. They will all know me, from the least to the greatest. I will forgive them for turning away from me, and I will welcome them home," says the Lord.

Wonder & Share 💡

▶ I wonder what good plans God had for Israel and Judah.
▶ What makes you dance for joy?
▶ What promise for the future would you want to hear from God?

Pray 💬

Make your own instruments as needed! Tap two spoons together. Put some dried beans or pasta in a sealed container and shake it. Tap a plastic container with unsharpened pencils to make a drum. Play your instrument as you say a joyful prayer of thanks.

Peace Path 🌅

I Am Special

God has a special plan for you—a plan for your good. I wonder what it is! Know that God's love for you will never end!

✍ **PAGE 170**

Speak to the Bones

EZEKIEL 37:1-14

THE PROPHET EZEKIEL also spoke about the time when God would bring the people of Judah back home from exile in Babylon. This was Ezekiel's vision from God:

"God's Spirit brought me to a valley of dry bones. Everywhere I looked, all I could see was bones. God asked me if the bones could live. Only God could know that. God told me to speak to the bones:

'Dry bones, listen to God! God will wrap you with muscles and skin. God will breathe new life into you.'

I heard a rattling noise. The bones came together! Muscles and skin covered them, but there was no breath in them.

God told me to speak to the wind and say:

'Blow from north, south, east, and west. Breathe life into these dead bodies so they can live.'

The wind blew. The bodies came to life and stood up, a vast crowd!

God said, 'The people of Judah are like these dead bones. They have lost hope. They think they are cut off from me. But I will set them free and bring them back home to the land of Israel. I will put my Spirit within them to give them life and breath. Then they will know that I, the Lord, keep my

Wonder & Share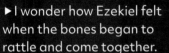

▶ I wonder how Ezekiel felt when the bones began to rattle and come together.

▶ Imagine God's Spirit breathing life into you.

▶ Have you ever been discouraged or lost hope? What comforts you in a hard time?

Pray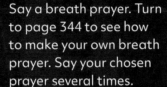

Say a breath prayer. Turn to page 344 to see how to make your own breath prayer. Say your chosen prayer several times.

Peace Path
God's Spirit Moves

In Ezekiel 37, the Hebrew word *ruach* means "breath," "wind," and "spirit" (either a person's or God's).

God promised to put breath into the bones so they could live. In Genesis 2, God also breathed life into Adam, the first created person.

PAGE 182

Bow or Burn

DANIEL 3

AFTER KING NEBUCHADNEZZAR of Babylon destroyed Jerusalem, he ordered his palace master to choose young men from wealthy families of Judah and teach them literature and languages. Three of the chosen men were Shadrach, Meshach, and Abednego. After three years of training, they were very wise and became part of the king's court.

King Nebuchadnezzar made a huge golden statue. He called together all the leaders and people to dedicate the statue.

His herald told all the people, "When you hear the sound of the horn, pipe, zither, lyre, harp, and flute, you must all bow down and worship the gold statue. If you do not, you will be thrown into the furnace of flaming fire."

The music played. All around them, people bowed down to the statue. But Shadrach, Meshach, and Abednego stood tall. They did not bow down.

When the king heard about this, he went into a rage and called the three men before him. "Is it true that you did not bow down to my golden statue? I will give you another chance. When the music plays, bow down or I will have you thrown into the furnace."

Shadrach, Meshach, and Abednego said, "We cannot worship a statue. We only worship God. We don't know if God will rescue us from the furnace, but we will not serve your gods or bow down to your statue."

The king was even angrier! He had the furnace heated seven times its normal heat. He had his strongest guards tie up the three men and throw them into the furnace.

But then the king was shocked! He said to his servants, "Didn't we tie up three men and throw them into the furnace?"

They replied, "Yes, O king. It is true." But there were four men in the furnace, not three, and they walked around freely.

The king called, "Shadrach, Meshach, and Abednego, servants of the Most High God, come out!" Everyone gathered around in amazement. The three men were not hurt! Their clothes and hair were the same as before. They did not even smell like the fire.

The king said, "Blessed be the God of Shadrach, Meshach, and Abednego, who sent an angel to save them from the fire! These men did not obey my law, but they trusted in God."

Wonder & Share

▶ I wonder why the king wanted people to bow down to the statue.
▶ Why can it be hard to do the right thing when other people are doing something wrong?

Pray

Ask an adult to light a candle as you pray, as a reminder that God protected Shadrach, Meshach, and Abednego in the fiery furnace. Ask God to protect you as you go from place to place this week.

Peace Path

God Is Amazing

What amazes you about this story? Imagine you are Shadrach. How would you tell this story to your friends? What would you say about God?

PAGE 224

Muzzled

DANIEL 6

THE PERSIANS defeated Nebuchadnezzar, the king of Babylon. King Darius became the new king in his place. There were 120 governors in his kingdom. King Darius chose three people to be in charge of the governors. One of them was Daniel. Daniel was such a great leader that the king planned to put Daniel in charge of the whole kingdom.

The other leaders were jealous. They wanted to get Daniel in trouble, so they tried to find something wrong with Daniel's work. But Daniel was honest and faithful.

What else could they do? They knew that Daniel loved God and prayed every day. So they went to the king and said, "O King Darius, may you live forever! Make a law that for 30 days, people can only pray to you. If someone breaks the law, throw that person into the den of lions." King Darius made the law.

Daniel knew about the law. But still he knelt by his open window three times a day to pray and praise God, just as he had always done.

The leaders caught Daniel praying and went straight to the king. They said, "O King Darius, may you live forever! Didn't you make a law that for 30 days people can only pray to you? Daniel, one of the highest leaders in the land, is ignoring your law. He continues to pray to God three times every day."

The king was very upset. He did not want to throw Daniel to the lions. For many hours, he tried to figure out how to rescue Daniel. But the law could not be changed. So Daniel was thrown into the den of lions. King Darius said, "May your God, whom you follow so faithfully, save you." A stone was placed over the entrance to the den.

The king went back to the palace. He could not sleep all night.

As soon as the sun rose, the king ran to the den of lions, shouting, "Daniel, did your God save you?"

"Yes," said Daniel. "God sent an angel to shut the mouths of the lions."

The king was so happy! He brought Daniel out of the den. Then the king wrote to all peoples and nations of every language in the world:

"It is my decree that all people should follow the God of Daniel:

For God lives forever!
    God delivers and rescues,
doing signs and wonders
    in heaven and on earth,
saving Daniel
    from the power of the lions."

Daniel continued to be a wise leader under King Darius, and then under King Cyrus of Persia.

Wonder & Share ☼

▶ I wonder how Daniel felt as he prayed, knowing that he was breaking the king's law.
▶ Share a brave thing you have done.

Pray ☺

Prayer was a daily habit for Daniel. Pray like he did! Look out a window as you pray and praise God three times today.

Live It ☀

Daniel was honest and faithful in his work. Think about the work you need to do this week, such as schoolwork, chores around the house, or practicing an instrument. Do your very best with each job!

Return to Jerusalem

EZRA 1, 3, 6

MANY YEARS after King Nebuchadnezzar had destroyed Jerusalem, the people of Judah were still living in Babylon. But then, King Cyrus of Persia sent a decree to everyone in the kingdom:

"The Lord God of heaven has made me the ruler of all kingdoms of the earth. God has chosen me to build the Lord a holy temple in Jerusalem. All people from Judah are free to go back to Jerusalem and build this temple. Anyone who wants to stay here in Babylon must help provide money, goods, and animals for those who want to return for this holy task."

Many families of Judah, as well as the priests and Levites, felt that God wanted them to help rebuild the temple. They got ready to go. All their neighbors gave them silver, gold, supplies, animals, and other gifts. Even King Cyrus took out the gold and silver bowls, knives, and chalices that King Nebuchadnezzar had stolen from Jerusalem years ago. King Cyrus had them counted and given back to Prince Sheshbazzar of Judah. The prince brought the vessels to Jerusalem, along with the exiled people who had been living in Babylon.

In the second year after the people returned to Jerusalem, Zerubbabel and Jeshua led the people in rebuilding God's temple. As they laid the foundation, the priests praised God with trumpets. The Levites played cymbals, sang, and praised God, saying:

"For the Lord is good,
 the Lord's kindness is forever."

People shouted with great joy as the foundation was laid. But many of the old priests, Levites, and family leaders cried loudly, because they remembered the first temple that had been destroyed years ago. The noise was so loud that people could not tell the weeping from the joyful shouts.

After many years, the people completed the temple. It was time to celebrate! The priests, Levites, and all the rest of the returned exiles had a celebration to honor the new temple. They sacrificed 100 bulls, 200 rams, 400 lambs, and 12 goats to God. They chose priests and Levites to serve in the temple, just as God had told Moses. With great joy, they celebrated the Passover feast together for seven days. They sacrificed the Passover lamb as God had taught them years ago in Egypt.

God brought the people of Judah back from Babylon to their home in Jerusalem, just as God had promised through the prophets. God was faithful, turning their sadness into joy.

Wonder & Share 💡

▶ King Nebuchadnezzar had taken gold and silver vessels from the temple many years ago. I wonder why King Cyrus decided to give them back.

▶ Share a happy memory and a sad memory.

Pray 💬

Celebrate! Express a joyful prayer using instruments and songs. Close with a prayer like the one the Levites prayed: *Lord, you are good and kind to us forever. Amen.*

Dig In 📖

Trace the time from the destruction of the temple to its rebuilding on the Old Testament Timeline on pages 358–359. Because so many years had passed, the young people and children had never seen Jerusalem. Imagine coming into the city for the first time!

Nehemiah's Example

NEHEMIAH 5

WHEN THE PEOPLE OF JUDAH returned to Jerusalem from exile in Babylon, the city was in ruins. Nehemiah the governor helped the people begin rebuilding Jerusalem, but trouble arose. People came to Nehemiah with their problems.

One said, "We have large families and there is not enough food for everyone. We have to sell our fields, vineyards, and homes just to buy grain!"

Another said, "We've had to borrow money so we could pay the king's tax. Our children have been enslaved, our vineyards and fields have been taken, and we can't do anything about it."

Nehemiah felt angry about how they were being treated. He thought it over, then called together the leaders and said, "We bought back all family members who were enslaved in other countries. Now, you're selling more people into slavery again!"

The nobles and officials were quiet. They knew this was true.

Nehemiah went on: "What you're doing is wrong. We need to live so that people know we follow God. I am part of this too. I am lending money and grain. But we must not demand payment. Give the people's fields, vineyards, and homes back. Don't cheat them anymore!"

The leaders said, "We will give it back and not ask any more of them." The whole community shouted, "Amen" and praised God.

But one official paused and said, "The former leaders forced the people to pay 40 silver coins a day and buy food for the governor. Aren't you going to do that too?"

Nehemiah said, "I could do the same thing since I am governor, but I respect God and will not do that. It is too hard for the people."

For the whole 12 years that Nehemiah was governor, he did not take his people's food, their land, or their silver. Every day he fed 150 Jewish people and their leaders, as well as visitors from other lands.

Wonder & Share

▶ I wonder why there was not enough food for everyone.
▶ Why did Nehemiah feel angry? How was his anger helpful? How can you use your anger in positive ways?

Pray

When the people realized that they were doing something wrong, they followed Nehemiah's lead and made different choices. Say an "I'm sorry" prayer. Tell God about a mistake you've made and ask God to forgive you. Then say aloud, "God loves me and forgives me!"

Practice Peace

How did Nehemiah care for the people around him? What could you do if a friend came to you and said, "Someone is being mean to me" or "I am being treated unfairly"?

Esther's Secret

BOOK OF ESTHER

KING AHASUERUS OF PERSIA planned a banquet for all the people of his kingdom. He wanted to show everyone how rich he was, so he decorated the marble columns with beautiful curtains. He put gold and silver couches on elegant floors that were made from costly stones, marble, and mother-of-pearl. The wine was served in gold goblets.

On the last day of the banquet, King Ahasuerus sent for Queen Vashti. He wanted everyone to look at her and see how beautiful she was. But Vashti refused to come. She did not want to be put on display. The king was furious. He was in charge. She should obey him, he thought. So he removed her as queen.

King Ahasuerus sent his servants to find the most beautiful woman in the land to be his new queen. Many young women were taken to the palace, including a young Jewish woman named Esther. Esther was living with her uncle Mordecai, who had adopted her when her parents died. Before Esther left for the palace, Mordecai pleaded, "Promise me that you won't tell anyone that you are Jewish. Something bad could happen to you." Esther promised.

When she was brought before the king, he liked Esther more than all the other women and crowned her as queen.

A man named Haman was in charge of all the king's officials. The king ordered all his servants to bow down to Haman. Everyone did this—except Esther's uncle Mordecai. Mordecai told the king's servants, "I am not Persian. I am Jewish. That is why I don't bow down to Haman."

Haman was furious and wanted revenge. He decided to try to kill all the Jews in the Persian Empire. Haman lied to the king, saying, "The Jews do not obey your laws. You should destroy them all." The king agreed and sent out an order: "On the 13th day of the 12th month, all Jewish men, women, and children are to be killed."

When Mordecai heard this, he tore his clothes and put on sackcloth, which Israelites wore in times of mourning. He went through the city weeping loudly. He said to Esther, "Beg the king to spare our people. You are queen, but that does not mean you will be safe. Perhaps God has made you queen for such a time as this."

Esther knew that anyone who approached the king without his permission could be killed. Yet she replied to Mordecai, "Gather all the Jews and pray and fast for me for three days. Then I will go to the king, even though I may die."

On the third day, Esther put on her royal robe and entered the throne room. But the king was not angry. He reached out his golden scepter toward her and said, "What upsets you? What do you want? I will give you anything you want, even half of my kingdom."

Esther said, "I would like to invite you and Haman to a special dinner." Haman and the king came to Esther's feast. The king offered again to give her anything she wanted. Esther told him, "I want you to save me and my people from our enemy. That is my only wish."

"Who is this enemy?" the king demanded. Esther pointed at Haman. The king was furious and had Haman killed immediately. He gave Esther everything that had belonged to Haman. He made Mordecai one of his officials and gave him Haman's royal ring.

The king gave Esther and Mordecai permission to make a new law to save their people. A new decree went out to the whole land: "On the 13th day of the 12th month the Jews are allowed to defend themselves against any army that attacks them."

When the Jewish people won the battle, they feasted and celebrated. They gave money to people who needed it and shared food with each other.

Pray 💬

Set the table for a special feast, just like Esther did for the king. Pray one of the meal prayers on page 344 before you eat.

Practice Peace 🕊️

Esther asked her family and friends to pray for her. The next time you are having a hard time, ask someone to pray for you.

Wonder & Share 💡

▶ Have you ever said no when something made you uncomfortable, like Vashti did? How did people respond?

▶ I wonder what gave Esther the courage to go to the king, even knowing that she might die.

▶ Tell about someone you know who spoke up for what was right.

Job and the Whirlwind
BOOK OF JOB

JOB LIVED IN THE LAND OF UZ and served God faithfully. He had seven sons and three daughters, many houses, and thousands of animals. Job was a rich and great man.

One day a messenger came to Job with terrible news: "Enemies destroyed your cattle and donkeys!"

Another messenger came and said, "Fire from heaven killed your sheep!" A third messenger arrived: "Bandits stole your camels and killed your servants!"

Then a fourth messenger came with the worst news of all: "Job, your sons and daughters were feasting when a great wind struck the house and killed everyone inside."

Job tore his robe in grief, shaved his head, and fell to the ground. Despite his terrible losses, Job did not turn away from God. He worshiped God, saying:

"I entered my mother's womb with nothing,
 I exit this world with nothing.
 Blessed be the name of the Lord."

After this, Job became sick with painful sores all over his body. He had to scrape them with a piece of broken pottery. Job's body and heart ached. Still, he did not curse God.

Job's three friends, Eliphaz, Bildad, and Zophar, came to comfort Job. He did not even look like himself anymore because he was hurting so much. Eliphaz, Bildad, and Zophar cried loudly for their friend. Then for seven days and nights, Job's friends sat with him in his silent grief.

After a week Job's friends spoke, trying to teach Job lessons about why the terrible things happened. Eliphaz and Bildad said, "You must have done something wrong." Zophar said, "God must be punishing you."

Job did not agree. He said, "My life is in God's hand. Ask the animals and birds. They will tell you. Ask the plants and trees. They know it too. Only God gives life and breath to every creature."

Later, Job wondered if God had forgotten him. Were his friends right? Was God punishing him?

Then God spoke to Job from a great stormy whirlwind:

"Who is this who speaks without knowledge?
Where were you when I created the earth?
   Tell me, if you understand.

Who measured the earth
or laid its cornerstone
    when the morning stars
    all sang together?
Who blocked the sea with doors,
    when it gushed from my womb,
when I made the clouds its clothing,
    and thick mist its swaddling cloth?
Do you open the storehouses of snow
    or bring rain in the desert?
Do you give the horse its strength?
    Does the eagle fly at your command?
I am the Lord All-Powerful,
    and I created you."

Job said to God:

"I know you can do all things.
I spoke but did not understand,
    wonders too great for me to know.
Before I had heard of you,
    now my eyes have seen you.
Therefore, I take back my words,
    and return to silence and lament."

Then the Lord spoke to Job's friends: "You have not spoken rightly of me, and you were wrong in your lessons to Job. Make a sacrifice to me, and Job will pray for you."

Job's friends followed God's command, and Job prayed for them. His family and friends came, bringing gifts of gold and silver. They ate bread, grieved, and comforted Job.

In time, the Lord returned Job's riches and livestock. The Lord blessed him again with a new family. He gave his three daughters special names that meant "Dove," "Cinnamon," and "Horn of Eyeshade." Job lived many years, long enough to see his grandchildren, great-grandchildren, and even great-great grandchildren.

Wonder & Share

▶ I wonder why Job's friends sat with him in silence for seven days.
▶ Who has comforted you when you were sad or in pain? What can you do when you notice someone else is having a hard time?

Pray

Lament means "expressing great sadness about something bad that has happened." That's what Job was doing in this story. What makes you feel sad? Tell God about this sadness with your own prayer of lament.

Peace Path
Nature Trail

Draw a whirlwind picture that shows the parts of nature God spoke about to Job. Add your favorite animals and plants to the picture. Thank God for creating and caring for the whole earth.

PAGE 212

Road to Nineveh

BOOK OF JONAH

GOD CALLED TO JONAH and said, "Get up, go to the great city of Nineveh, and tell the people that they are doing things that are wrong." Instead of going to Nineveh, Jonah boarded a boat sailing in the opposite direction, toward Tarshish.

A huge storm arose. Wind blew and howled, waves crashed against the ship, and water poured across the deck. At any moment the ship would break apart. The sailors were terrified. They threw cargo overboard to try to lighten the load of the ship. They prayed to their gods, begging for safety.

Down below deck, Jonah had fallen sleep. The captain shook him awake: "What are you doing! Get up! Call on your god to save us."

The sailors got together. Who was to blame? They cast lots, and the lot fell to Jonah. Jonah said, "I am a Hebrew, but I am fleeing from God who made the sea and land. Throw me into the sea and the storm will stop."

The sailors did not want to do this. They tried rowing to shore instead, but the storm just got worse. Finally, they picked Jonah up and threw him into the sea. The wind stopped. The water became calm.

God sent a great fish to swallow Jonah. Jonah spent three days and nights inside the fish. He prayed:

"I called out to you, Lord,
    and you answered me.
You heard my voice.
    You flung me into the sea.
The waters flowed over me.
    Seaweed wrapped around my head.
Down, down, down I went.
    But you brought me up from the pit.
Just when I thought I would drown,
    my prayer came to you.
And now with great thanks,
    I will keep my promise.
You are the only one who has power to save."

God spoke to the fish, and it spit Jonah onto dry land.

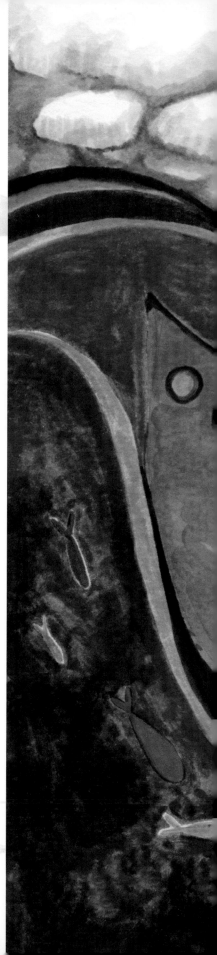

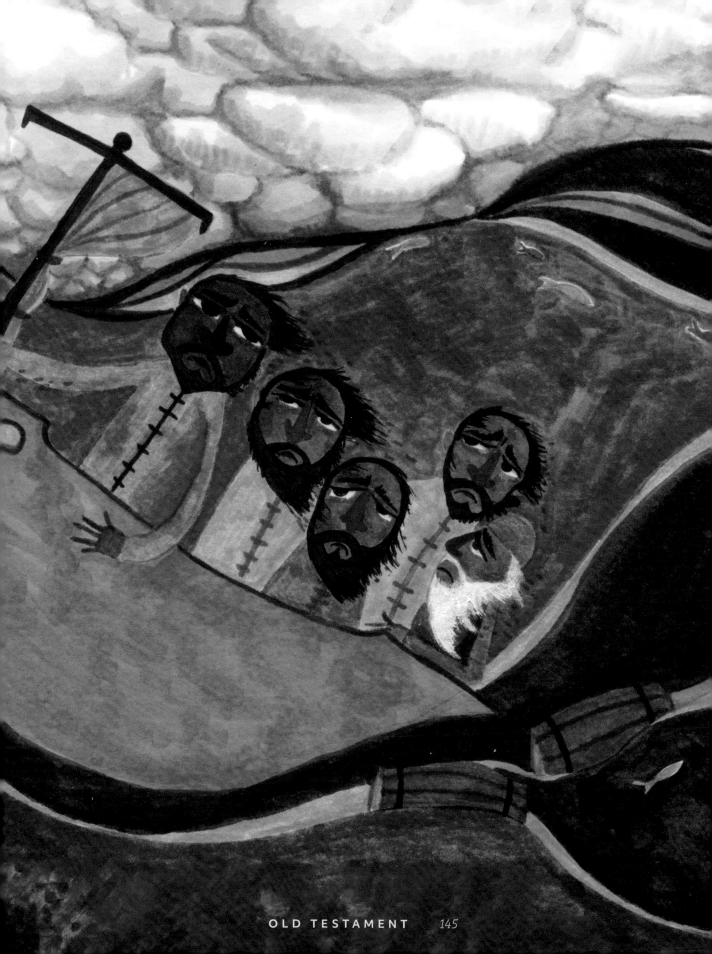

Again, God said to Jonah, "Get up, go to the great city of Nineveh, and tell the people that they are doing things that are wrong." This time Jonah went. As he walked through the city, he called out, "In 40 days, Nineveh will be destroyed." And all the people trusted in God. They put on sackcloth and did not eat to show their sorrow. Even the king put on sackcloth and sat in ashes.

The king declared, "All people must pray and turn back from the wrong they have done. Perhaps God will have mercy and not destroy us." God had compassion and changed course. God did not destroy the city.

Jonah was bitter. He prayed, "I knew this would happen. It's why I fled to Tarshish. I knew that you are a merciful and loving God, slow to get angry and filled with kindness. You don't like to punish anyone. I can't stand it. And now, take away my life."

Jonah went out of the city. He made a shelter and sat under it to see what would happen to the city. God sent a plant to grow up and give him shade. Jonah was happy. But at dawn the next day, a worm attacked the bush and it died.

As the sun rose, God sent a violent wind. Jonah grew so hot and faint that he wanted to die. God asked, "Is it right for you to be angry about the bush?" Jonah said, "Yes, angry enough to die."

God said, "You care about a bush that you did not plant or grow, a bush that only lived for one night. Nineveh is a great city of 120,000 people who do not know right from wrong. And there are so many animals. Should I not have compassion on the people and animals?"

Wonder & Share ☀

▶ I wonder why Jonah wanted Nineveh to be punished instead of forgiven.
▶ Share about a time it was hard to do the right thing.

Pray 💬

Slowly repeat Jonah's prayer several times: *"You are a merciful and loving God, slow to get angry and filled with kindness. Amen."*

Dig In 📖

Nineveh was the capital of the Assyrian Empire. It was located by the Tigris River in what is now Iraq. For nearly 50 years, Nineveh was the largest city in the world. Much of the city was ruined in the Battle of Nineveh in 612 BCE.

Song of Shelter

PSALM 91

THE ONE WHO DWELLS in God's shelter will be at rest.
  I trust in the Lord, who is my refuge and fortress.
God will save me from enemies and illness.
  God is like a bird, covering me with feathers,
protecting me under God's wings.

I won't fear the dangers of the night
  or the terrible things that happen during the day.
I trust in God, who is my refuge and dwelling place.
  No disaster will come near my tent.
God's angels will lift me up.

God says, "I will rescue you and protect you.
  I will answer you when you call.
I will be with you in trouble.
  I will save you and give you long life."

Wonder & Share

▶ I wonder how it feels to be covered with the feathers of a bird.
▶ Share about a time you felt scared and a time you felt safe.

Pray 💬

Wrap yourself in a blanket, imagining God's wings of protection around you. Tell God your fears.

Peace Path
I Need Comfort

Hard and scary things happen. We can bring our concerns to God, knowing that God will always be with us. Try one of the "Peace Inside" ideas on page 350 the next time you feel sad or scared.

☞ **PAGE 236**

Song of Creation

PSALM 104

PRAISE THE LORD, O my soul!
  God, you are very great!
You wear light like a majestic coat.
  The heavens are like a tent.
The clouds are your chariot.

You send water rushing down into the valleys,
  giving drink to every animal.
The birds sing by the streams.
  You make grass grow for animals to eat.
The earth brings forth food for people.

Birds build their nests in the trees you made.
  The stork has a home in the fir tree.
The mountains are for the wild goats.
  The rabbits hide safely among the rocks.

You made the sun, the moon, and the darkness.
  Animals come creeping out at night.
The lions roar, needing food from you.
  People go out to work until evening.

How wonderful are your works, O Lord!
  The earth is full of your creatures.
Everything on earth looks to you for food.
  When you open your hand,
all creatures are filled with good things.
  When you take away their breath,
they return to the dust.

May your glory last forever!
  I will sing to you my whole life.
As long as I live, I will praise you.
  You are very great!
Praise the Lord!

Wonder & Share

▶ Imagine God's open hands filling the whole world with good things.
▶ What are your favorite animals? Where do they live? What food does God provide for them?

Pray

Praise God for creation. Name animals, birds, insects, and plants in your prayer. If you enjoy drawing, make a creation picture that includes your favorite things.

Peace Path
Let It Grow

God provides food for animals and people. What crops grow near you? Learn about the farmers and workers who tend the fields and gather the food.

PAGE 210

Song for Traveling

PSALM 121

I LIFT MY EYES to the hills.
Where does my help come from?
My help comes from God,
the great Creator of heaven and earth.

God will not let your foot slip.
God will not fall asleep
but will always watch over you,
just as God watches over Israel.

God is like a shade tree,
protecting you from the bright sun.
God will keep you safe in the moonlit night.

God will keep you from harm,
watching over your life, now and forever.

Wonder & Share

▶ Imagine God as a beautiful tree giving you shade on a hot day.

▶ I wonder what you do when you feel unsafe.

▶ What songs would you like to sing on a family trip?

Pray

Choose a morning prayer and evening prayer from page 342 to say today. If possible, find a place where you can see the sun and then the moon as you pray.

Dig In

Psalms 120–134 are all Songs of Ascent. People traveling to worship God in Jerusalem sang these short songs. Look at the map on page 368 to see the many hills that surround Jerusalem.

Song of Justice

PSALM 146

PRAISE THE LORD!

Praise the Lord, O my soul!
I will sing and praise God my whole life.

Do not trust in princes and leaders.
They cannot save you. Their plans die with them.
Happy are those who hope in the Lord,
the great Creator of heaven and earth,
for the Lord is always faithful.

God makes things right for those who are mistreated
and gives food to people who are hungry.
God sets prisoners free
and gives sight to those who cannot see.
God lifts up people who feel the weight of the world
and loves when people do what is right.
God watches over the foreigners
and cares for orphans and widows.

The Lord reigns forever,
for all generations.
Praise the Lord!

Wonder & Share 💡

▶ The psalmist names many things God does. What are they? I wonder how God does those things.

▶ Which line of the psalm do you like best? Why?

Pray 💬

Name things you are happy about or grateful for. After each one, say "Praise the Lord!"

Practice Peace 🍃

How could you lift up someone who feels weighed down by difficult things?

Song of Praise

PSALM 148

PRAISE THE LORD!
Praise the Lord from the highest heaven.
Praise the Lord, all you angels,
every being, high and low.

Praise the Lord, sun and moon.
Praise the Lord, all you bright stars.
God created you, beautiful earth,
so praise the name of the Lord!

Praise the Lord, from the seas,
all you great creatures of the deep.
Even the rain, snow, fire, and hail
do as God commands.

Praise the Lord, mountains and hills,
fruit trees and cedar trees.
Praise the Lord, wild animals,
creeping things, and flying birds.

Kings and all peoples,
rulers from around the world,
all people, young and old,
let us praise the Lord together.

God's name is high over all,
God's glory is above earth and heaven.
God has raised up the faithful people.
Praise the Lord!

Wonder & Share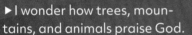

▶ I wonder how trees, mountains, and animals praise God.
▶ Write another verse for this psalm. Which animals, plants, or other nature items will you include?

Pray 💬

What can you praise God for today? Choose one of the Ways to Pray from pages 340–341 to express your praise.

Live It ☀️

Go outside and enjoy God's beautiful world! Use all your senses to notice the ways that creation is praising God.

NEW TESTAMENT

A New Beginning

JOHN 1:1-18

IN THE BEGINNING was Jesus the Word.
The Word was with God.
The Word was God.

All things were made through Jesus the Word.
All of life and light came from him.
Light shines in the darkness and cannot be overcome.

God sent John into the world.
He was to tell others about Jesus, the Light of the World,
so that all people might believe.

Jesus the Word put on flesh and made a home with us.
Many people did not understand who he really was.
But he gave everyone power to become children of God.

The law was given through Moses.
Everlasting love and truth came through Jesus,
the One who made God known to the world.

Wonder & Share

▶ Imagine a light that never goes out.
▶ I wonder where Jesus would make a home in our neighborhood.

Pray

Find a flashlight or battery-operated candle. Turn off the lights. As you pray, turn on the flashlight or candle to remind you that Jesus, the Light of the World, hears your prayer.

Dig In

The Ten Commandments were part of the law that God gave to Moses on Mount Sinai. Read the commandments on page 62. To see what John told others about Jesus, read page 182.

Elizabeth and Zechariah

LUKE 1:5–25

HUNDREDS OF YEARS after the time of the prophets, there lived a priest named Zechariah. Zechariah and his wife, Elizabeth, were followers of God. They had grown old and had no children.

One day, Zechariah was chosen to go into the temple to burn incense on the altar. All the people waited outside, praying. An angel of the Lord appeared to Zechariah, right next to the altar. Zechariah was filled with fear.

But the angel said, "Do not be afraid, Zechariah. God has heard your prayers. Your wife, Elizabeth, will have a son. Name him John. He will bring you joy, and many others will celebrate his birth. He will be filled with the Holy Spirit and will be great in God's sight. John will help the people return to serving God."

Zechariah said, "How can this be? My wife and I are too old."

The angel said, "I am Gabriel. I stand in the presence of God. God sent me to bring you this good news, and yet you do not believe. You will now be unable to speak until the day John is born."

The people outside began to wonder why Zechariah had been gone so long. When he came out, he could not speak!

After finishing his service at the temple, Zechariah went home to Elizabeth. Things happened just as the angel Gabriel had said. Elizabeth became pregnant. For five months she stayed at home. "God has done this great thing for me," she said. "No longer will people look down on me for not having a child."

Wonder & Share 💡

▶ I wonder why the angel Gabriel came to Zechariah inside the temple.

▶ The angel brought good but unexpected news. What good or surprising news have you heard recently?

Pray 💬

Zechariah and Elizabeth prayed for a very long time before their prayer was answered. Say the same prayer every day this week.

Dig In 📖

The altar of incense was in the Holy Place of the temple. The altar was made of acacia wood and covered in gold. Priests usually only offered incense once in a lifetime. Find the Holy Place on the diagram of Herod's temple on page 367.

Mary's Song

LUKE 1:26–56

ELIZABETH HAD A COUSIN named Mary. Mary lived in the small village of Nazareth in Galilee. She was engaged to Joseph.

The angel Gabriel was sent by God to tell Mary an important message. Gabriel said, "Mary, you are blessed! God is with you." Mary was confused. What could this mean?

The angel said to her, "Do not be afraid, Mary. God loves you and has a message for you. You will have a baby and name him Jesus. He will be holy and will be called the Son of God. God will make him king, just like David. Jesus' kingdom will never end."

Mary asked, "How can this be?"

The angel replied, "It will happen by the Holy Spirit and by the power of God. Your cousin Elizabeth is pregnant with a son, even though she is very old. Nothing is impossible for God."

Mary said, "Here am I, willing to serve God. Let it happen just as you said." The angel left her.

Mary hurried to Elizabeth's home. When Mary went inside, the Holy Spirit filled Elizabeth. Elizabeth said to Mary, "When I heard your greeting, my baby jumped for joy within me. God has blessed you and your child. You are blessed for believing God's promises."

Mary sang,

> **"With my whole being**
> **I praise the Lord!**
> **I am filled with joy**
> **because of God my Savior.**
> **The Mighty One cares for me**
> **and has done great things for me.**
>
> **God scatters the proud,**
> **takes strong rulers off their thrones,**
> **and has humble people lead.**
> **God gives food to the hungry,**
> **sending the rich away with nothing.**
> **God will keep the promises**
> **made to Abraham and Sarah's family forever!"**

Mary stayed with Elizabeth for three months and then went back home to Nazareth.

Wonder & Share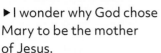

▶ I wonder why God chose Mary to be the mother of Jesus.

▶ God's love for Mary filled her with joy. What gives you joy?

Pray 💬

Read the first paragraph of Mary's song (in bold) aloud several times as your prayer. Then read Hannah's prayer on page 74. How are they similar?

Dig In 📖

Elizabeth lived in the hill country of Judea, possibly in the city of Hebron. This was about 80 miles / 130 kilometres from Nazareth, where Mary lived! Find these places on the map of Israel on page 368.

What Is His Name?

LUKE 1:57-80

SEVERAL MONTHS LATER, Elizabeth gave birth to a son. On the eighth day, their friends and family came together to celebrate and see what the baby would be named. They thought his name would be Zechariah, just like his father. But Elizabeth said, "No, he is to be called John."

The friends and family were surprised. "No one in your family has that name," they said. They called Zechariah over. What name would he give the baby? Zechariah still could not speak, so he got a clay tablet and wrote, "His name is John." Everyone was amazed!

Immediately, Zechariah could speak again! He was filled with the Holy Spirit and began to praise God saying:

> "Blessed be the Lord God,
>   who has raised up a Savior
>   from the house of David.
> The Lord has set us free from our enemies,
>   and from the power of all who hate us.
> Now we can serve God without fear."

Zechariah went on to bless his son, John:

> "You, my child, will be the prophet of the Most High God.
>   You will prepare the way for the Lord.
> Because of God's great love,
>   dawn will shine upon us,
> to give light to all who are in darkness,
> to guide us into the way of peace."

News about these amazing events spread throughout the hill country of Judea. All who heard it wondered, "Who will this child become? Surely God is with him."

Wonder & Share

▸ Imagine Elizabeth holding baby John for the first time.
▸ Do you know the story of your name? Who chose it? Does it have a special meaning?

Pray

Part of Zechariah's prayer was a blessing for his son. Pray a blessing for someone in your family. You could also write or draw the blessing and give it to the family member.

Practice Peace

Zechariah spoke about the "way of peace." Be on the lookout for words of peace. You might find them during conversations; in songs, videos, and books; and on posters, signs, or even billboards! Peace is all around us.

Joseph's Dream

MATTHEW 1:18–25

LONG AGO, God made a promise through the prophet Isaiah, saying:

"A virgin will give birth to a son.
   He will be called Emmanuel,
   which means "God is with us.""

This is how God's promise came true:

A young woman named Mary was engaged to Joseph. He was from King David's family. Before they were married, she found out she was going to have a baby by the Holy Spirit. Joseph followed God's ways and did not want people to shame Mary. So he decided to call off the wedding quietly.

But then an angel appeared to him in a dream, saying, "Joseph, son of David, do not be afraid to have Mary as your wife. Her baby is from the Holy Spirit. Name him Jesus, for he will set people free from sin."

When Joseph woke up, he did what the angel said. Mary and Joseph got married. She gave birth to a son, and they named him Jesus.

Wonder & Share

▶ Imagine an angel coming to you in a dream. I wonder what the angel might tell you.

▶ How can we know that God is with us?

Dig In 📖

Jesus is a form of the Hebrew name *Joshua*, which means "God saves."

Pray

Say a partner prayer. One person prays for a friend or family member. The other person responds by saying, "God is with _____ (*name of friend or family member*)." Then switch parts.

Born in Bethlehem

LUKE 2:1-7

IN THOSE DAYS, Emperor Augustus sent out a decree that all people must return to their family's hometown to be counted. Joseph was from King David's family. He was engaged to Mary, and she was about to have a baby.

The two of them set out from Nazareth to go to Bethlehem, the city of David. They traveled for many days through Galilee, Samaria, and the hill country of Judea. Finally, they came to Bethlehem. The city was filled with other people who had also come there because of the emperor's decree.

Mary and Joseph tried to find somewhere to stay, but there was no room in an inn. They could only find shelter in a place meant for animals. There, Mary gave birth to a son and named him Jesus. She wrapped him in strips of cloth and laid him in a manger.

Wonder & Share 💡
▶ I wonder how Mary felt on the long trip to Bethlehem.
▶ What are three ways to celebrate the birth of Jesus?

Pray 💬
Pray for babies you know or for babies around the world, that they will be healthy, safe, and loved.

Peace Path
I Am Special
Every baby is unique and special. What was unique about Jesus' birth? What is special about you and your birth?

📎 **PAGE 252**

Shepherds, Songs, and a Stable

LUKE 2:8-20

SHEPHERDS LIVED IN THE FIELDS near Bethlehem, watching over their sheep by night. An angel of the Lord appeared to them. God's glory shone around them. They were terrified!

But the angel said, "Do not be afraid. I am bringing you good news, which will fill your hearts with joy: today in the city of David, a Savior has been born. He is Christ the Lord. Here is the sign: You will find a child wrapped in strips of cloth and lying in a manger."

Suddenly, there were many angels around them. The angels praised God, saying, "Glory to God in heaven. Peace to all people on earth."

When the angels went back to heaven, the shepherds said to each other, "Let us go to Bethlehem and find this child who the angels told us about." They hurried to Bethlehem, searching until they found Mary, Joseph, and baby Jesus. Jesus was wrapped in strips of cloth and lying in a manger. The shepherds told Mary and Joseph what the angels said about Jesus. Mary treasured all these things in her heart.

Then the shepherds left, telling everyone they met about what happened. All the people were amazed. The shepherds returned to the fields, praising God for all they had seen and heard.

Wonder & Share

▶ Imagine God's glory shining around you.

▶ Share an exciting thing that happened to you. Whom did you tell first?

Pray 💬

Praise God by singing or dancing to a happy song! Wave streamers, ribbon, or strips of cloth as part of your prayer.

Practice Peace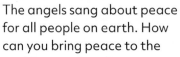

The angels sang about peace for all people on earth. How can you bring peace to the world around you?

Anna and Simeon

LUKE 2:21-40

EIGHT DAYS AFTER JESUS WAS BORN, his parents named him Jesus, just as the angel had told Mary to do. Then they went to the temple in Jerusalem to present him to God as instructed by the Law of Moses.

Simeon lived in Jerusalem. He followed God with his whole heart, and the Holy Spirit rested on him. God had promised Simeon that he would see the Savior before he died. But Simeon was very old now. Would God's promise come true after so many years of waiting?

One day, God's Spirit led Simeon to the temple. There, he saw Mary, Joseph, and baby Jesus. Simeon gently took Jesus in his arms. He praised God, saying:

> "Lord, now I can rest in peace,
>   for I have seen the promised Savior!
> This child will be a light for the whole world,
>   bringing salvation for all people."

Simeon blessed Joseph and Mary. Then he said to Mary, "Your son will bring hope to many people, but some will reject him and his teachings. This will be very painful for you, like a sword piercing your heart."

The prophet Anna was also in the temple that day. She was 84 years old and never left the temple. She fasted and prayed, both day and night. When she saw baby Jesus, she praised God and told everyone about Jesus the Savior.

After Mary and Joseph did all that the Law required, they took Jesus to their home in Nazareth. Jesus grew strong and was full of wisdom. God's blessing was on him.

Wonder & Share

▶ I wonder how long Simeon waited for God's promise to come true.

▶ What would you say to bless a new baby?

Pray 💬

Both Simeon and Anna praised God for Jesus. Choose one of the "Ways to Pray" from pages 340–341. Do that as you praise God for good things that happened to you this week.

Practice Peace 🕊

Simeon told Mary that her son would be rejected. How do you respond when someone is mean to you? What could you do if a person you care about is being rejected or treated badly?

Follow That Star

MATTHEW 2:1–12

ONE NIGHT, a bright star rose in the sky. It shone brighter than all the other stars. Magi from the East saw the star and said to each other, "A king has been born!" They set out to follow the star and find the king.

Far away in the land of Israel, Herod was king. After a long trip, the magi came to King Herod in the city of Jerusalem and said, "Where is the child who has been born king of the Jews? We followed his star, and we want to worship him."

King Herod was scared about this news, as were all the people in Jerusalem. King Herod called the priests and scribes together. "Where is this king supposed to be born?" he asked them.

They replied, "This is what the prophet Micah says:

'You, Bethlehem, may be small,
    but you are not the least in the land of Judah.
A great ruler will come from you,
    who will be a shepherd for Israel.'"

King Herod secretly sent for the magi to find out when the star had risen in the sky. Then he said to them, "Go to Bethlehem and find this child. When you have found him, send word to me. I want to worship him too." But Herod was not telling the truth. He did not want to worship the child. He wanted to get rid of the child so that he could still be king.

The magi followed the star until it stopped over a house in Bethlehem. They were filled with joy. When they went inside, they saw the child Jesus with his mother, Mary. They knelt and worshiped Jesus, then gave him special gifts of gold, frankincense, and myrrh.

That night, an angel appeared to the magi in a dream, warning them not to go back to King Herod. They returned to their own country by another road.

Wonder & Share 💡
▶ I wonder how Mary felt when the magi came.
▶ What is a special gift you have given or received?

Pray 💬
Kneel as you pray, like the magi did when they worshiped Jesus.

Live It ☀
Draw three gift boxes. In each box, write or draw something you could do to honor Jesus.

Escape to Egypt

MATTHEW 2:13-23

AFTER GIVING GIFTS of gold, frankincense, and myrrh to young Jesus, the magi left Bethlehem. They did not tell King Herod they had found the king they were looking for—Jesus. They went home another way.

When Herod found out, he was furious. He called his soldiers together and said, "I am the true king. Get rid of all the children in Bethlehem, since one of them will try to become king in place of me."

That very night, an angel came to Joseph in a dream, saying, "Get up quickly. Take Jesus and Mary and flee to Egypt. King Herod is going to search for Jesus to kill him. Stay in Egypt until I tell you."

So Joseph got up, took Jesus and Mary by night, and made the long trip across the desert to the land of Egypt. They lived safely in Egypt until King Herod died.

Then an angel came to Joseph in a dream again, saying, "Get up, take Jesus and Mary, and go back to the land of Israel."

When they came to Judea, they found out that Herod's son was ruling that area. They were afraid to stay there. Another angel came to Joseph, telling him to travel back to the town of Nazareth. Mary, Joseph, and Jesus made a home there and lived in peace and safety.

Wonder & Share

▶ I wonder how Jesus and his family were treated in Egypt.
▶ God sent an angel to guide Jesus' family to safety. Share about people who help keep you safe.

Pray

Jesus and his parents were refugees, which meant they had to flee their own country because of danger. Pray for the many refugees around the world today who have to live far from their homes.

Practice Peace

It must have been frightening to flee for another country in the middle of the night. Which of the "Peace Inside" ideas from page 350 would help you in that situation?

My Father's House

LUKE 2:41–52

JESUS LIVED WITH HIS PARENTS in Nazareth. Every year they went to Jerusalem to celebrate the festival of Passover. When Jesus was 12 years old, he and his parents went to Jerusalem for the festival, along with their family and friends.

After the festival was over, it was time to go home. Mary and Joseph set out with their family, friends, and neighbors. But Jesus stayed behind in Jerusalem. His parents did not know. They thought he was in the group of travelers.

A day went by. Mary and Joseph started worrying about Jesus.

They asked Jesus' friends, "Is Jesus with you?" No, he was not.

They asked the aunts and uncles, "Have you seen Jesus?" No, they had not.

They asked the neighbors, "Did Jesus pass by here?" No, not today. Where could he be?

Mary and Joseph rushed back to Jerusalem to find him. They searched everywhere they could think of—in the market, at the inn, along the city walls, by the pools, near King Herod's palace. But Jesus was nowhere to be found.

After three days, they went to the temple. There he was! Jesus was listening to the teachers and asking them questions. Everyone was amazed at what he knew and understood.

Mary hurried over to him and said, "Child, we were so worried! Why have you done this? We have been looking everywhere for you."

Jesus said, "Why were you looking for me in other places? Didn't you know I would be here in my Father's house?"

Mary and Joseph did not understand what he meant.

Jesus and his parents went back home to Nazareth together. Mary treasured this time with him. Jesus grew from a boy into a man. He was wise, and the people loved him.

Wonder & Share ☀

▸ I wonder what questions Jesus asked the temple leaders.
▸ Who helps you learn new things?

Pray 💬

Ask God questions as you pray. See if you can come up with six questions that begin with each of these words: *who, what, when, where, why,* and *how*.

Dig In 📖

Jesus was the son of Mary and Joseph, but he was also the Son of God. That's why Jesus said he was in his Father's house at the temple. Jesus also called himself Lord, Messiah, Christ, Teacher, Good Shepherd, the light of the world, the true vine, and the gate.

My Beloved Son

MARK 1:1–11; LUKE 3:21–22

THE BEGINNING OF THE GOOD NEWS of Jesus Christ, the Son of God:
The prophet Isaiah wrote:

> "See, I am sending a messenger
>   to prepare your way.
> A voice will cry from the wilderness:
>   'Prepare the way of the Lord,
> Make straight paths!'"

John, the son of Elizabeth and Zechariah, lived in the wilderness. He wore clothing made from camel's hair, with a leather belt around his waist. He ate locusts and wild honey. He was called John the Baptist.

People from the whole countryside of Judea, and all the people of Jerusalem, came to hear John preach by the Jordan River. John cried out, "Prepare the way of the Lord! Make straight paths. Turn away from doing wrong and follow the ways of God." The people confessed their sins, and John baptized them in the river.

One day he told the crowd, "There is One coming who is more powerful than I am. I am not even worthy to untie his sandals. Today I have baptized you with water. He will baptize you with the Holy Spirit."

Jesus came from his home in Nazareth to be baptized. John said, "You should not come to me to be baptized. I need to be baptized by you!"

But Jesus said, "No, it is right for you to baptize me."

So John agreed. He baptized Jesus in the river. As Jesus came up out of the water, the heavens opened. The Spirit came down upon him in the form of a dove. A voice from heaven said, "You are my Son, the Beloved. I am well pleased with you."

Wonder & Share

▶ I wonder why John preached in the wilderness instead of in a building.

▶ I wonder how Jesus felt when the voice from heaven said, "You are my Son, the Beloved."

▶ Whom do you love? Who loves you?

Pray

The people who came to be baptized *confessed* the things they had done wrong. Tell God something you have done wrong. Then pour water slowly over your hand as you say, "God forgives me."

Peace Path
God's Spirit Moves

The Holy Spirit came down on Jesus in the form of a dove, which is a symbol of peace. Hundreds of years before Jesus' baptism, the prophet Isaiah called him the Prince of Peace.

PAGE 194

Jesus and the Tempter

LUKE 4:1-13

AFTER JESUS WAS BAPTIZED by John in the Jordan River, the Spirit led him into the wilderness. He did not eat anything for 40 days and nights. By that time, he was desperately hungry.

The tempter came to him, saying, "If you are the Son of God, tell this stone to become a loaf of bread."

But Jesus refused. Instead he said, "The scriptures say, 'We do not live by bread alone. The word of God also gives us life.'"

The tempter took Jesus to the top of the temple in Jerusalem and said, "If you are the Son of God, throw yourself down from here. For the scriptures say, 'God will send angels to protect you. You will not even hurt your foot on a stone.'"

But Jesus did not do that. Instead he said, "The scriptures also say, 'Do not test the Lord your God.'"

The tempter took Jesus to a very high mountain. He showed him all the kingdoms of the world and said, "I will give you the glory and power of these kingdoms. Just bow down and worship me."

But Jesus would not do that. Instead, he said, "Go away from me! The scriptures say, 'Only worship the Lord your God.'"

The tempter left him, and angels came to care for him.

Wonder & Share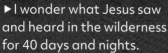

▶ I wonder what Jesus saw and heard in the wilderness for 40 days and nights.

▶ Think of a time you felt tempted to do something wrong. Who or what helped you to do the right thing?

Pray

The scriptures that Jesus quoted are all from the book of Deuteronomy in the Old Testament. Say the prayer from Deuteronomy called the Shema. It is in bold print on page 62.

Dig In

Forty is an important number in the Bible. It rained for 40 days when Noah was in the ark (page 24). The Israelites wandered in the desert for 40 years (page 60). Jesus was in the wilderness for 40 days.

Synagogue, Scroll, and Stories

LUKE 4:14–30

JESUS, FILLED WITH THE POWER OF THE HOLY SPIRIT, went back to Galilee. He began to teach, and everyone praised him. When he came to his hometown of Nazareth, he went into the synagogue. The people gave him the scroll of Isaiah. Jesus unrolled it and read:

"The Spirit of the Lord is upon me
and has anointed me
    to bring good news to those who are poor,
        to set the prisoners free,
    to give sight to people who are blind,
        to free all who suffer,
to proclaim the year of God's blessing."

He gave the scroll back and sat down, saying, "Today, this scripture has come true."

The people were amazed! They said, "This is Joseph's son, from our town. Listen to how well he speaks!"

But Jesus said, "I know you want me to do amazing things like I did in other places. But prophets say hard things too and are not welcome in their hometown. Long ago, there was no rain here in Israel for more than three years. People were starving, including many widows. But God sent the prophet Elijah far away to help a widow in the town of Zarephath. There were also many people in Israel who had the skin disease of leprosy. But God sent the prophet Elisha far away to care for a man with leprosy who lived in the country of Syria."

Just as Simeon had predicted when Jesus was a baby, the crowd grew angry at Jesus' teaching. They forced him to the edge of town so they could throw him off a cliff! But Jesus walked through the crowd and went away.

Wonder & Share ☀

▶ Jesus' stories showed God's love for people outside of Israel. I wonder why that made the people of Nazareth feel so angry.
▶ What would be good news for someone who doesn't have what they need?

Pray 💬

Pray for people you love. Then pray for people who live in far-away places who are different from you.

Dig In 📖

Jesus reminded the people about the prophet Elijah and the widow of Zarephath. Read their story on page 100. Find Nazareth, Zarephath, and Syria on the map on page 368.

Follow Me

MATTHEW 4:17–22; MARK 1:16–20

WHEREVER HE WENT, Jesus said, "God's kingdom is here! Change your heart and mind!"

One day, Jesus was walking by the Sea of Galilee. Gentle waves lapped against the shore, and a breeze blew. Birds flew overhead, calling out to each other.

Jesus saw two brothers, Simon Peter and Andrew, in a fishing boat. They were throwing their nets into the sea. Jesus called to them, saying, "Follow me! I will show you how to fish for people." Immediately, they left their nets and followed Jesus.

Jesus kept walking. He saw two more brothers, James and John. They were in a boat with their father, fixing their nets. "Follow me," Jesus said, "I will show you how to fish for people." They said goodbye to their father, left their boat behind, and followed Jesus.

Wonder & Share ⋅💡

▶ I wonder what it means to "fish for people."
▶ Tell about a time you made a new friend.

Pray 💬

Make a prayer boat! Find a container that will float. Write or draw pictures of your prayers on small pieces of paper and put them in the "boat." Float your prayer boat in the bathtub or sink.

Live It ⋅💖

The brothers helped each other fish, fix the nets, and take care of the boat. Work together on a project with someone in your family this week.

Cast Your Nets

LUKE 5:1–11

JESUS WAS STANDING on the shore of the Sea of Galilee. People crowded around him, wanting to hear the word of God. He saw two fishing boats. He got into the boat belonging to Simon Peter and asked him to row a little way out from shore. Jesus began to teach the crowd again from the boat.

When he was done, Jesus said to Simon, "Row the boat out into the deep water. Let down your nets to catch some fish."

Simon said, "Lord, we worked hard all night and did not catch anything. But since you are telling us, we will do it."

They cast their nets into the deep water. Fish swarmed the nets until the nets began to rip apart! Simon and Andrew called their friends in another boat to help them. Together, they filled both boats with fish until the boats started to sink! They were all surprised at the amazing catch of fish.

Simon fell on his knees in front of Jesus. "Lord, go away from me! I do many bad things."

But Jesus told him, "Do not be afraid. From now on you will bring in people instead of fish."

They rowed their boats to shore, left everything, and followed Jesus.

Wonder & Share

▸ Imagine a net suddenly filled with fish.
▸ What kind of job or activity are you happy to help a friend with?

Pray

Cut out paper fish. Write the name of a person or draw a picture of a person you want to pray for on each fish.

Peace Path
Water Wonders

Find the Sea of Galilee on the map on page 368. It is the lowest freshwater lake in the world, providing drinking water for many people, and fish to eat. The three main types of fish in the lake are musht (also called Saint Peter's Fish), biny, and Kinneret sardines.

 PAGE 192

Wedding Wonders

JOHN 2:1-11

JESUS, HIS MOTHER, AND HIS DISCIPLES were at a wedding in the village of Cana in Galilee. It was a joyful celebration. People danced, laughed, ate, and drank together.

But then the wine ran out. Jesus' mother said, "Jesus, there is no more wine."

Jesus replied, "Mother, it is not yet time to show who I am."

His mother told the servants, "Do whatever Jesus says."

There were six large stone jars that people used to wash themselves. Each jar could hold 20 to 30 gallons of water. Jesus told the servants, "Fill the jars to the top with water, then take some to the person in charge of the wedding feast." The servants did this.

The person in charge tasted it. It wasn't water. It was delicious wine! He called the bridegroom over and said, "Most people serve the best wine first. But you have saved the best wine for last!"

This was the first amazing sign that showed Jesus' glory. His disciples believed in him.

Wonder & Share 💡

▶ I wonder what Mary thought Jesus would do when the wine ran out.

▶ Wedding celebrations in biblical times often lasted a full week. Guests brought food or drink to share. What food would you bring?

Pray 💬

What is the most amazing thing you have seen? Praise God for amazing things in the world around you.

Peace Path 🌄
Water Wonders

Jesus showed his glory and power using something as simple as water! In what ways is water important for people and the earth?

👉 **PAGE 218**

A Nighttime Visitor

NICODEMUS SERVED AS A LEADER of the Jewish people. He wanted to talk with Jesus, who was in Jerusalem for the Passover festival. He waited until nightfall to visit Jesus in secret.

"Teacher," Nicodemus said, "We know you come from God because of the amazing things you can do. God must be with you."

"It is true," Jesus answered. "You cannot see God's kingdom unless you are born from above."

Nicodemus was surprised. "What do you mean?" he asked Jesus. "How can anyone be born after they have already grown old? A person can't return to their mother's womb."

"No one can enter the kingdom of God without a mother *and* God's Spirit giving birth to them," Jesus explained. "What is born from a body is another body. What is born of the Spirit is spirit. Don't be surprised I said you must be born from above. When the wind blows, you can feel it, but you don't know where it comes from or where it goes. That's what it is like to be born of God's Spirit."

"How can this be?" Nicodemus asked.

"I'm telling you about what I see and know," Jesus responded. "Trusting in me is the way of eternal life."

Jesus continued, "God loves the world so much and sent the beloved Son into the world. Whoever believes in God's Son will have eternal life. God did not send the Son to punish the world but to save it. I'm here to be a light. People who do wrong want to hide from the light. But people who do what is true come into the light without fear."

Wonder & Share 💡

▶ I wonder why Nicodemus went to meet Jesus in secret.
▶ I wonder how it feels to be born of God's Spirit.
▶ What questions would you like to ask Jesus?

Pray 💬

Nicodemus came to Jesus at night. Choose one of the evening prayers from page 342 to pray before bed.

Peace Path

God's Spirit Moves

Jesus compared God's Spirit to the wind. On the next breezy day, go outside and feel the wind blowing on you. Or make a paper fan to create wind. Imagine God's Spirit all around you.

PAGE 294

The Samaritan Woman

JOHN 4:4-42

JESUS AND HIS DISCIPLES were traveling from Judea to Galilee. They came to the city of Sychar in Samaria. The disciples went into the city to buy food. Jesus was tired, so he sat down at the well. It was noon.

A woman came to the well to get water. Jesus said, "Please give me a drink."

The woman was shocked and said, "You are a Jewish man, and I am a Samaritan woman. Why would you ask me for something to drink?"

Jesus said, "If you knew who I was, you would be asking me for living water."

She said, "You don't have a bucket, and this well is very deep. Where would you get this living water?"

"When you drink the water from this well, you will be thirsty again," Jesus said. "But if you drink the water I give, you will never be thirsty again! The living water will be like a gushing spring inside of you, giving you new life for all eternity."

The woman said, "Please give me this water!"

Jesus then told the woman what he knew about her: She had been married five times and was now with a different man. The woman was amazed that Jesus knew those things.

Then the woman told Jesus what she knew: "I can tell you are a prophet," she said. "The Messiah is coming! He will teach us all things."

Jesus said, "I am the Messiah."

The woman left her water jar and hurried back to the city. She told everyone, "Come and meet a man who told me everything I have ever done! Could he be the Messiah?" The people went to find Jesus.

Meanwhile, the disciples wanted Jesus to eat something. But he said, "I do not live by bread alone. I am fed by doing the work that God called me to do."

Many Samaritans in the city believed in Jesus because of what the woman told them. They said, "Truly, Jesus is the Savior of the world."

Wonder & Share 💡

▶ Many Jews and Samaritans hated each other. Jesus was a Jew. I wonder why he chose to go to Samaria and talk to Samaritans.

▶ Share two things that you know about Jesus.

Pray 💬

Take sips of water before, during, and after your prayer. Imagine Jesus' living water filling you.

Dig In 📖

Find the city of Sychar on the map on page 368. It is in the region of Samaria. Samaritans and Jews both followed God but believed different things. Samaritans worshiped God at Mount Gerizim rather than at the temple in Jerusalem.

Jesus the Healer

MARK 1:29-45

ON THE SABBATH, Jesus went to the synagogue and began to teach. The people were amazed by what they saw and heard. There was something different about this man. News about Jesus spread throughout Galilee.

After leaving the synagogue, Jesus, James, and John went home with Simon and Andrew. Simon's mother-in-law was in bed, sick with a fever. Jesus took her by the hand and helped her up. The fever left her, and she made a meal for them.

That evening, crowds of people came to Simon and Andrew's home. They brought many loved ones who were sick and in need of healing. Jesus healed them of all kinds of diseases.

Very early in the morning before the sun rose, Jesus went to a deserted place to pray alone. His disciples searched everywhere for him. When they finally found him, they said, "Everyone is looking for you!"

Jesus said, "Let's go to nearby towns so I can tell the good news there too. This is why I have come."

Jesus continued to travel throughout Galilee, preaching and healing the sick. A man with a skin disease called leprosy came to Jesus and knelt at his feet, saying, "I know that you have the power to heal me, if you want to."

Jesus felt love for the man. He touched him and the leprosy disappeared. Jesus said, "Do not tell anyone what I have done for you. Just go show yourself to the priest." But the man was so happy that he could not help himself! He told everyone. He told so many people that Jesus couldn't go into a town without crowds following him. So Jesus stayed out in the country. Still people came to him from all around.

Wonder & Share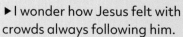

▶ I wonder how Jesus felt with crowds always following him.
▶ Share about a time someone in your family was sick. What care did they need?

Pray 💬

Jesus went out to pray by himself early in the morning. Choose one of the morning prayers from page 342.

Dig In 📖

Leprosy is a painful skin disease. Jewish law said touching a person with leprosy would make you "unclean." But Jesus touched the man anyway, and he was healed!

Five Friends

MARK 2:1–12

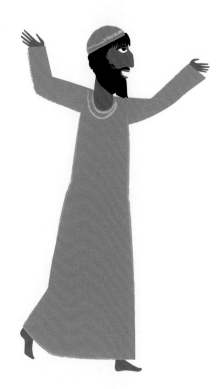

WHEN JESUS WENT BACK TO CAPERNAUM, people heard that he was at home and came to see him. They filled the entire house. There was not even room to stand near the door.

Jesus was teaching them when four more people came, carrying a man who was unable to walk. They wanted Jesus to heal their friend, but the crowd was so big that they could not reach him. The four friends carried the man up the steps to the roof.

The friends dug through the roof and lowered the man into the room, right in front of Jesus! Jesus saw their faith and said to the man, "Child, your sins are forgiven."

The scribes were shocked because they knew the Law of Moses. "How can he say that?" they whispered to each other. "Only God can forgive sins. By saying this, he has broken our holy law."

Jesus saw them whispering and knew what they were saying. "Why are you asking these kinds of questions? Is it easier to say, 'You are forgiven,' or to say, 'Get up and walk?'"

Jesus wanted them to understand that his power to forgive was from God. So he said to the man, "Get up, take your mat, and go home." The man stood up, picked up his mat, and walked out in front of everyone. The people were amazed and praised God, saying, "We have never seen anything like this!"

Wonder & Share

▶ I wonder whose idea it was to dig through the roof. I wonder how other people felt about that plan.

▶ Share about a time you helped a friend.

Pray 💬

Pray for five friends. Hold up one finger for each friend as you pray.

Peace Path

Love Your Neighbor

Some people in this story were helpers, but others blocked the way to Jesus. They did not make room for the five friends to come to Jesus. I wonder why they kept them away. How can we welcome everyone in our homes, churches, and schools?

 **PAGE 230**

Calling Disciples

MARK 2:13–17; 3:13-19

JESUS WENT TO THE SEA OF GALILEE and taught the crowd that gathered around him. As he continued on, he saw Levi sitting at a booth collecting taxes. Jesus said, "Follow me." Levi got up and followed Jesus.

Jesus and his disciples went to eat at Levi's house. Tax collectors and sinners who were followers of Jesus joined them. The scribes and Pharisees did not like this. "These are bad people," they said to Jesus' disciples. "Why is Jesus eating with them?"

Jesus heard them and said, "People who are healthy don't need a doctor. Look around the table. These are the people I came to call."

Later Jesus went up a mountain. He chose 12 of his many followers to be his disciples: Peter (the name he gave to Simon), the brothers James and John (whom he called "Sons of Thunder"), Andrew, Philip, Bartholomew, Matthew, Thomas, James son of Alphaeus, Thaddaeus, Simon, and Judas Iscariot. He gave them power to teach and heal.

Wonder & Share ✦

▶ I wonder how each disciple felt about being chosen by Jesus.

▶ Why do people sometimes avoid each other?

Pray 💬

Jesus chose 12 disciples. List 12 people you would enjoy spending time with every day. Then say a prayer for those special people.

Live It ☀

Jesus ate with unexpected people. Invite someone new to eat with you this week.

Blessed Are . . .

MATTHEW 5:1–16

JESUS WENT UP A MOUNTAIN with his disciples and began to teach them, saying:

"Blessed are the poor in spirit—
they need others, and others need them—
for they will have a heavenly home.
Blessed are those who are deep in sadness,
for they will be comforted and given strong defense.
Blessed are those who are humble and gentle;
the earth will be theirs.
Blessed are those who hunger for justice and right living;
they will be filled.
Blessed are those who do loving kindness;
they will also receive loving kindness.
Blessed are those who have a clear heart and mind,
for they will know God.
Blessed are the peacemakers,
for they will be called children of God.
Blessed are those who are hurt for seeking justice,
for they will have a heavenly home.
Blessed are you when people are mean and speak lies about you because you follow me. You can have joy even in those hard times, because God has a heavenly reward for you. Remember, people also hurt the prophets of God in the past.

You are the salt of the earth that keeps food from becoming rotten and thrown out.

You are the light of the world. You shine like a city on a hill, or a lamp on a tall stand. Let your light shine, so that others will see your good works and praise God in heaven."

Wonder & Share 💡
▶ I wonder which "blessed are" statement means the most to you right now.
▶ How can you let your light shine at home, in your neighborhood, and with your friends?

Pray 💬
Say the Lord's Prayer on page 345, which is also part of Jesus' Sermon on the Mount.

Dig In 📖
The nine "blessed are" statements are called the Beatitudes. They are part of a longer teaching by Jesus known as the Sermon on the Mount. The sermon is three chapters long! Check out Matthew 5–7 to read the whole thing.

Love Your Enemies

LUKE 6:20-36

JESUS AND HIS DISCIPLES left the mountain and made their way down to the plain. A large crowd of people traveled from across Judea, from Jerusalem, and from the coast to hear Jesus and to be healed from sickness. Everyone tried to touch Jesus, and his power healed them all.

Jesus looked at them and said:

"Blessed are you who are poor. The kingdom of God belongs to you.

Blessed are you who feel hungry now. You will be filled.

Blessed are you who weep now. You will laugh.

Blessed are you when people hate or exclude you because of me. When this happens, you can jump for joy because this is the same thing that happened to the prophets of God.

But misery will come to you who are rich. You have already received your comfort.

Misery will come to you who are full now. You will be hungry.

Misery will come to you who laugh now. You will weep.

Many people say, 'Love your neighbor and hate your enemy.' But I say to you: Love your enemies. Do good things for them. Speak words of blessing when people speak words of hate. Pray for them. If someone hurts you, turn to peace and not violence. Give to everyone who asks you. Treat others the way you want to be treated."

Jesus continued, "Even people who do wrong love the people who love them. When you are kind to someone who is kind to you, should you get extra praise? That is easy to do. But love your enemies and give to people without expecting anything back from them. This is what makes you children of God.

When people are ungrateful or do wrong things, God remains kind. Show mercy like God shows mercy."

Wonder & Share

▶ I wonder how people become enemies.

▶ Sometimes Jesus' teachings make people feel uncomfortable. Is there a part of this teaching that makes you upset or is hard to understand?

Pray 💬

Think of a time you did not get along with someone. Pray for that person.

Peace Path

Love Your Enemies

What ideas did Jesus give for how to love an enemy? What other ideas do you have?

PAGE 320

Parable of the Builders

MATTHEW 7:24–29

JESUS ENDED HIS LONG SERMON with this story:

"Anyone who hears these words of mine—and lives by them—is like a wise builder. The wise builder builds a house on a strong foundation of rock. The rain falls; floods come; wind blows and beats against the house. But the house will not fall since it was built on solid rock.

Anyone who hears my words but does *not* live by them is like a foolish builder. The foolish builder builds a house on sand. The rain falls; floods come; wind blows and beats against the house. And the house falls with a great crash since it was built on shifting sand."

The crowds were amazed at Jesus' teaching. They knew they could trust his words.

Wonder & Share

▶ I wonder why someone would build a house on sand.
▶ Tell about a time you were safe during a storm.

Pray

Pray using Jesus' words. Read the Lord's Prayer aloud from page 234 or 345.

Live It

Right before telling this story, Jesus taught his followers about loving their enemies, praying, and giving. He did not want them just to *think* about his teachings, but to *live* by them. Turn back one page. Read the paragraph that begins, "Many people say . . ." Choose one of those actions to do this week.

Parable of the Sower

MARK 4:1-20

A LARGE CROWD gathered around Jesus as he was teaching by the Sea of Galilee. He got into a boat and taught the crowd from there. Jesus told them a story:

"Listen! A farmer went out to plant seeds. Some seeds fell on the path. The birds came and ate them. Some seeds fell on rocky ground where there was not much soil. They grew quickly. But the sun came out, and the tiny plants dried up because they did not have roots. Some seeds fell among the thorny plants. They began to grow, but the thorns choked the plants. A few seeds fell on good soil. They grew and grew, producing 30, 60, or even 100 times more than what was planted."

After the crowd went away, Jesus explained the story to his disciples:

"I will help you understand the mystery of God's kingdom. What the farmer is spreading is the message about the kingdom of God. The seeds on the path are people who hear God's message, but then Satan takes it away. The seeds among the rocks are those who joyfully receive the message. But as soon as trouble comes along, they fall away because they do not have deep roots. The seeds among the thorns are people who hear the message but get caught up in the worries of this life. They want to get rich and have many things. God's message gets choked out, producing nothing. The seeds sown in the good soil are people who hear the message, accept it, and bear 30, 60, or even 100 times more than what was planted."

Wonder & Share

▶ I wonder who the farmer is in Jesus' story.
▶ Who spreads God's message of love and hope today?

Pray 💬

Draw a prayer. Draw a seed at the bottom of the page. For each thing you pray for, draw another part of the plant. For a flower, draw the stem, add leaves, and then add flower petals. For a tree, draw the trunk, add branches, and then add leaves.

Peace Path

Let It Grow

What do plants need to grow? In the Bible story, what got in the way of some plants growing? What helps you grow?

This is the end of the path! Go to **PAGE 16** to choose another peace path.

Parable of the Mustard Seed

MATTHEW 13:31–32

JESUS TOLD THE PEOPLE A PARABLE:

"The kingdom of God is like a mustard seed—the smallest of all seeds. Someone digs into the rich soil of a field, plants the seed, and waters it. The warm sun shines down.

The seed slowly grows and grows and grows. The roots spread deep and wide. The trunk grows thick and strong. Branches reach toward the sky. Leaves appear and yellow flowers blossom on the tips of the branches. The tiny seed becomes a great tree!

Then birds come from near and far—different colors, shapes, and sizes. They build nests in the branches. Mother birds lay their eggs. They all sing together to welcome the baby birds."

Wonder & Share 💡
▶ I wonder why God's kingdom starts small.
▶ Which part of a tree do you like best? How many trees can you name?

Pray 💬
Entire forests around the world are being cut down all at once. Pray for the many people, plants, and animals that are affected by this.

Peace Path
Nature Trail
What do you know about birds? How do birds help the earth? Find out what colors these birds are: cardinal, parrot, goldfinch, raven, dove, oriole, robin, parakeet.

👉 **PAGE 332**

Parable of the Yeast

MATTHEW 13:33-35

JESUS TOLD ANOTHER STORY:

"The kingdom of heaven is like yeast used to make bread. A woman scoops out three measures of flour—enough for over 100 loaves of bread! She pours the yeast into the flour. She stirs and stirs until the yeast is evenly spread through all the flour. After adding more ingredients, the woman forms the mixture into soft dough. With time, the dough rises. Then she bakes it into delicious bread that can be shared."

Jesus only spoke to the crowd using stories. This fulfilled what the prophet said long ago:

"I will speak in parables;
I will tell you the things that have been hidden
since the beginning of the world."

Wonder & Share 💡
▶ I wonder what the woman did with all the bread.
▶ Share about a time you worked hard to make something.

Pray 💬
Next time you eat a meal or snack, pray for a different person with each scoop of food you put on your plate.

Live It ☀
Make or buy a loaf of bread. Share it with a neighbor, friend, or even a stranger!

Treasure Parables

MATTHEW 13:44-48

JESUS TOLD THREE STORIES to help people imagine God's kingdom:

"The kingdom of heaven is like a treasure hidden in a field. Someone digs in the field, finds the treasure, and then covers it up again. Joyfully, the person sells everything to buy the field where the treasure is buried."

"The kingdom of heaven is like a merchant who is searching for fine pearls. When the merchant finds a pearl of great value, she sells everything she has and buys it."

"The kingdom of heaven is like a net that is thrown into the sea and catches fish of every kind. When the net is full, those who were fishing pull it ashore. They sit down and divide the fish, putting the good fish into baskets to keep.

Wonder & Share 💡

▶ What would you do if you found a buried treasure?

▶ I wonder what the merchant does with the pearl after selling everything to get it.

▶ What are three things that you treasure?

Pray 💬

A pearl is shaped like a ball. Search for round things in your home, such as marbles, balls, or oranges. Say a prayer each time you find one.

Dig In 📖

In biblical times and beyond, people often hid coins or other valuable things in pots or jars and then buried them in a field. A buried treasure belonged to whoever owned the field.

Storm at Sea

MARK 4:35–41

THAT EVENING, after telling the people many stories, Jesus said to his disciples, "Let's go across the Sea of Galilee." They got into the boat, leaving the crowd behind. Several other boats went with them.

A great storm arose. The wind howled. Waves beat against the boat, swamping it with water. But Jesus was in the back sleeping on a pillow! The disciples woke him up, saying, "Teacher, don't you care that we are about to drown?"

Jesus spoke to the wind and sea: "Peace! Be still!" The wind stopped and everything became calm. Jesus said to the disciples, "Why were you afraid? Don't you have faith in me?"

They were filled with great fear and said to each other, "Who can he be? Even the wind and the water do what he says!"

Wonder & Share 💡

▶ I wonder how Jesus' voice sounded when he said, "Peace! Be still!"

▶ Tell about a time you were in a storm. How did you feel? Pray for people who have gone through hard times because of a storm.

Pray 💬

Tell God a fear or worry you have. Then say Jesus' words: "Peace! Be still." Repeat with your other fears and worries.

Peace Path 🗺

Water Wonders

The Sea of Galilee is known for having sudden storms. Fierce winds can blow off the steep hills around the lake, causing large waves. Jesus calmed one of these storms, keeping his disciples from being harmed!

👉 This is the end of the path! Go to **PAGE 16** to choose another peace path.

Two Daughters

LUKE 8:40-56

AFTER JESUS CROSSED the Sea of Galilee, a great crowd was waiting for him. Jairus, a leader of the synagogue, came and knelt at Jesus feet. "Please come to my house," he begged. "My daughter is dying. She is only 12 years old. You must help her!" Jesus went to help, with the crowd following him.

In the crowd, there was a woman who had been sick for 12 years. She had spent all her money on doctors, but none of them had been able to help her. She moved through the crowd until she was close to Jesus. She reached out and touched the edge of his robe. Immediately she could feel in her body that she was healed!

Jesus stopped. "Who touched me?"

The people denied it, and Peter said, "People are crowding all around you and pushing you from every side!"

But Jesus said, "Someone touched me. I felt power go out from me."

The woman knelt at Jesus' feet, trembling in fear. She said to him, "I touched your robe, and right away I was healed!"

Jesus said, "Daughter, your faith made you well! Go in peace."

Just then, someone came from Jairus' house and said to Jairus, "Your daughter has died. Do not bother Jesus anymore."

But Jesus said, "Do not be afraid! Believe in me and your daughter will get well."

When they came to the house, Jesus, Peter, James, John, and the girl's parents went inside. Everyone was crying for her, but Jesus said, "Do not cry. She is not dead, only sleeping." They laughed at him; they knew she was dead.

But Jesus took the girl by the hand and said, "Child, get up!" Right away, she got up! Everyone was amazed! Jesus told her parents to give her something to eat and not to tell anyone what had happened.

Wonder & Share

▶ I wonder why the woman thought she would be healed just by touching Jesus' robe.
▶ I wonder how Jesus felt when people laughed at him. Has that ever happened to you?

Pray

Pray for people who are sick. Ask God to show you how to care for someone who is sick.

Art Spotlight

While Jesus lived in Israel thousands of years ago, he came to bring the good news of God's love to the whole world. The illustrator imagined that this story took place in Mexico. Imagine if Jesus came to heal people in a town or city near you!

Laura James

A Hungry Crowd

MARK 6:30-44

JESUS AND HIS DISCIPLES were tired and hungry. They left in a boat for a quiet place where they could rest and eat.

The crowd saw them leave and hurried to the place where Jesus was going. The crowd got there first!

Jesus got out of the boat and looked at the people with love. They were like sheep without a shepherd. He began to teach them many things.

That evening, Jesus' disciples said, "Send the crowds away so they can go buy food for themselves."

But Jesus said, "You feed them!"

The disciples were surprised. How could they possibly feed a crowd of 5,000 people? It would cost so much money!

Jesus said, "Go and see how much bread there is." The disciples found five small loaves of bread and two fish.

Jesus told the disciples to have the people sit down in groups of 50 and 100. He took the bread and fish, looked up to heaven, and blessed the food. The disciples passed out the food. Everyone ate until they were full. The disciples even gathered 12 baskets of leftovers!

Wonder & Share 💡

▶ The disciples were tired and wanted to rest in a quiet place. I wonder how they felt when they saw the crowd coming.
▶ What would you have done with the leftover food?

Pray 💬

As you pray, imagine Jesus looking at you with love.

Peace Path 🏃

God Is Amazing

How could five loaves of bread and two fish be enough to feed such a huge crowd? Not only was there enough food for everyone, there were also leftovers! What does this show you about God?

 **PAGE 250**

Throwing Stones

JOHN 8:1-11

JESUS TRAVELED up the Mount of Olives, a place where he sometimes went to pray and be with God. When Jesus came back to the temple, he began to teach those who gathered.

The leaders brought a woman to Jesus. The leaders wanted to trick Jesus. They hoped he would deny the law of Moses, so they could have him arrested. So they said, "Teacher, this woman was caught not being faithful to her marriage. The Law of Moses—the important words we live by—tells us to throw stones to kill people like her. What do you say?"

Jesus bent down and wrote words on the ground with his finger. The leaders continued to question him.

Jesus stood up straight and said, "If you have never done anything wrong, throw the first stone."

He bent down again to write on the ground, and one by one, the people who had accused the woman trickled away.

Jesus stood up again. He asked the woman, "Where are your accusers? Has anyone tried to punish or kill you?"

"There is no one," she answered.

"I won't punish you either," Jesus said to her. "Go on your way. From now on, don't do wrong again."

Wonder & Share

▸ I wonder what Jesus wrote on the ground.
▸ How would you feel if someone tried to get you in trouble?

Pray 💬

Find a stone that will fit in your hand. Grip it tightly. Tell God about a wrong thing you have done. Then slowly open your hand and set the stone down as you say, "God forgives me."

Practice Peace 🕊

Jesus used spoken and written words to make peace and keep the woman safe. Come up with a list of peacemaking words you can use.

The Good Shepherd

JOHN 10:1-18

JESUS WAS SPEAKING TO SOME PHARISEES. They were important Jewish leaders. He said, "I tell you, the one who enters the sheepfold by the gate is the shepherd of the sheep. Thieves try to sneak in by another way. The shepherd calls the sheep by name and leads them out. They follow the shepherd because they know his voice. They will not follow a stranger. They will run away because they do not know the stranger's voice."

The Pharisees did not understand what Jesus was saying. So he went on, "I tell you, I am the gate for the sheep. Those who came before me were thieves, but the sheep did not listen to them. I am the gate. Those who enter by me will be saved. They will be able to come into the sheepfold for safety and go out to the fields to eat and drink. A thief only comes to steal, kill, and ruin things. But I came to bring new life.

"I am the Good Shepherd. I will do anything to keep my sheep safe. I will even give my life for them. A person who is hired to watch the sheep will run away if a wolf comes. The hired person does not care about the sheep.

I am the Good Shepherd. I know my sheep and they know me, just like God knows me and I know God. I willingly give my life for the sheep; no one forces me to do it.

I will bring sheep from other places into my fold. They will listen to my voice. Then there will be just one flock and one shepherd."

Wonder & Share 💡

▶ Imagine you are a sheep following a shepherd to find food and water.

▶ Sheep know the sound of the shepherd's voice. How can we know when God is speaking to us?

Pray 💬

Jesus will bring sheep from many places to make one flock. Choose something to represent sheep, such as cotton balls or stuffed animal toys. Form them into a circle to make a "flock." Touch each "sheep" as you pray for a different person.

Peace Path 🌄
I Am Not Alone

Jesus knows you by name and cares for all your needs, just like the Good Shepherd cares for the sheep. Jesus will lead and comfort you.

 PAGE 240

Who Is My Neighbor?

LUKE 10:25-37

WHEN JESUS WAS TEACHING, people often asked him hard questions. Some people were just curious. Some were seeking answers because they wanted to follow him. But others wanted to get him in trouble.

A man came to Jesus and said, "What do I need to do to live forever? The law says I must love God with my heart, soul, mind, and strength, and love my neighbor as myself."

"Yes," said Jesus. "Do these things and you will live."

But this man wanted to test Jesus. "Who is my neighbor? Whom do I have to love?"

Jesus told him this story:

"A man was going from Jerusalem to Jericho. Thieves came along. They took the man's clothes, hit him, and left him to die.

A priest came down the road. He saw the hurt man. He crossed to the other side of the road and went away.

A Levite also came by and saw the man. He crossed to the other side of the road and went away.

A Samaritan came by and saw the man. His heart filled with love. He knelt down and put bandages on the man's wounds. He helped the man onto his donkey, took him to an inn, and cared for him. The next day he gave the innkeeper money and said, 'Take care of this man. I will be back soon and will pay for anything he needs.'"

Jesus then asked the man, "Who was a neighbor? Was it the priest or the Levite or the Samaritan?"

The man said, "It was the one who took care of the hurt man and showed him mercy."

Jesus said, "Go and be like that Samaritan."

Wonder & Share

▶ I wonder why the priest and Levite went by without helping.
▶ Share about a time you were a loving neighbor.

Pray 💬

Pray for people who have been hurt by violence.

Peace Path

Love Your Neighbor

What peacemaking actions did the Samaritan take? Look at the "Peace with Others" ideas on pages 352–353. The priest and Levite missed an opportunity to help. What can stop us from helping others?

👆 PAGE 248

Mary and Martha

LUKE 10:38–42

AFTER SOME TIME IN GALILEE, Jesus and his disciples traveled to Samaria and then toward Jerusalem. Crowds continued to gather wherever Jesus went.

Jesus came to the town of Bethany where his friends Martha and Mary lived. Martha invited him into their home. Martha's sister Mary sat at Jesus' feet as he talked, just like his other disciples did.

Martha worked and worked while Mary and Jesus talked. After awhile, Martha came to Jesus and said, "Don't you care that my sister has left me with all the work? Tell her to help me."

But Jesus said, "Martha, you are worried and busy with so many things. Only one thing is needed right now. Mary has chosen what matters most. It won't be taken away from her."

Wonder & Share 💡

▶ I wonder what Jesus and Mary talked about.
▶ What jobs need to be done at your home? Who helps?

Pray 💬

Draw a picture of your family. Pray for each family member as you draw.

Peace Path
Family Problems

Martha was frustrated with her sister. This happens a lot in families! What can you do when you are upset at someone in your family? Look at the "Peace with Others" ideas on pages 352–353.

📖 PAGE 242

Parable of the Midnight Visitor

LUKE 11:1-13

AFTER LEAVING MARY AND MARTHA'S HOME, Jesus was praying by himself. His disciples came to him and said, "Lord, teach us to pray like John the Baptist taught his disciples."

Jesus said, "When you pray, say:

> 'Father, holy is your name.
> Your kingdom come.
> Give us today the bread we need.
> And forgive us our sins,
> for we forgive others.
> And do not bring us to a time of trial.'"

Jesus went on to tell them a story: "Imagine that you go to your friend's house at midnight and say, 'Friend, people have come to visit me, and I do not have enough food to give them. Please share bread with me.'

But your friend says, 'Do not bother me! The door is locked, and my children are in bed with me. I cannot get up and give you anything.'

However, you need food. Won't you knock again and again? Since you do not give up, your friend will finally come and give you what you need.

So I tell you: Ask and it will be given to you. Search and you will find. Knock and the door will be opened for you. Everyone who asks will receive. Those who search will find. The door will open for those who knock. If your children ask for a fish, will you give them a snake? If your children ask for an egg, will you give them a scorpion? You know how to give good gifts to your children. Imagine how much more God will give the Holy Spirit to those who ask."

Wonder & Share 💡

▶ I wonder how many times the friend had to ask for food before getting help.
▶ What can help you stay strong when you feel like giving up?

Pray 💬

The prayer Jesus taught his disciples is often called the Lord's Prayer. Say it aloud as your prayer. It is in bold print.

Art Spotlight

The illustrator imagined that this parable happened near *Capilla del Cristo*, a small chapel built in the 18th century in Old San Juan, Puerto Rico. Imagine it happened near a church in your area. How can a church help people who need food?

Birds and Flowers

LUKE 12:22-34

THOUSANDS OF PEOPLE GATHERED, trampling on one another to get near Jesus.

Jesus said to them, "Do not worry about your life or what you will eat. Life is more than food. Look at the ravens. They do not plant crops. They do not put food in barns. But still God feeds them. Think of how much more God cares for you!

Do not worry about your body or what you will wear. There is more to the body than clothing. Look at the lilies, how they grow. They do not sew clothes for themselves. But even King Solomon in all his glory was not dressed like one of these. If God clothes the grass, which lives for only a short time, think of how much more God will clothe you!

Many people worry about food and clothing. But you do not have to worry about these things. God knows what you need. Instead turn your heart toward God, and these other things will be given to you as well.

You do not need treasures here on earth. Sell what you own and give the money away. Then you will have treasure in heaven, and no thief can steal it. Where your treasure is, that's where your heart is.

Wonder & Share 💡
▶ I wonder what worries you.
▶ The illustrator included birds and flowers found near her home in eastern Canada. What birds and flowers are near you?

Pray 💬
Write or draw a picture of one of your worries. Draw a flower or bird around your worry to remind you that God cares for you.

Peace Path 🌂
I Need Comfort

The next time you feel worried, choose one of the "Peace Inside" ideas from page 350 to do. What else helps you feel better?

✍ **PAGE 272**

Parable of the Great Dinner

LUKE 14:15–24

ONE SABBATH, Jesus was having dinner at the home of a Pharisee, one of the Jewish leaders. He told the dinner guests a story:

"Someone gave a great dinner and invited many people. When the food was cooked and everything was ready, the host sent a servant to tell the invited guests that it was time to eat.

The servant said to the guests, 'Come! Dinner is ready.' But they all made excuses.

The first guest said, 'I just bought a field and must go see it. I am sorry, but I won't be able to come.'

The second guest said, 'I bought five yoke of oxen, and I am going to try them out. I am sorry, but I can't come.'

The third guest said, 'I just got married and cannot come.'

The servant returned to the host with the news. The host became angry and said, 'Go into the town. Look up and down every street. Find people who are poor. Find people who can't walk or see. Tell them to come to my dinner. Don't miss anyone.'

The servant did this, but there was still room.

The host said, 'None of those who were first invited will eat this meal. So go back to the town. Search every road and alley. Bring everyone you can find. I want my house to be filled!'"

Wonder & Share

▶ Imagine the host's house filled with people eating, talking, and laughing together.

▶ Tell about a time you were invited to a special event like a birthday party. Have you ever been left out or *not* invited? How did you feel?

Pray 💬

The host's friends didn't come to the dinner, even though they said they would. Friends sometimes let us down, and we might feel angry, hurt, disappointed, or sad about it. Pray for your friends, even the ones who have let you down.

Live It ☀

Some of the people at the dinner could not walk or see. Get to know someone whose body works differently than yours.

Parables of the Lost

LUKE 15:1–10

ONE DAY, Jesus was talking with some tax collectors and some people who had done many wrong things. The scribes and Pharisees did not like this. They said, "Jesus welcomes everyone and even eats with them."

So Jesus told them two parables:

"Imagine you had 100 sheep. One evening, you count the sheep, only to discover that one is missing. Wouldn't you leave the 99 sheep in the wilderness and go look for the lost sheep? Wouldn't you keep looking and looking until you found it? Then you would carry the sheep home, call all your friends and neighbors, and say, 'I found my lost sheep. Let's celebrate!' Just like this, there is more joy in heaven for one person who turns from doing wrong to right than for 99 people who are already doing the right thing.

And if a woman has 10 coins and loses one, wouldn't she light a lamp, sweep the floor, and search carefully in every corner until she finds it? Then she will call her friends and neighbors and say, 'I found my lost coin. Let's celebrate!' Just like this, there is great joy in heaven whenever a person turns from doing wrong to right."

Wonder & Share

▶ The illustrator imagined this parable happened in Indonesia. I wonder how the shepherd and woman will celebrate finding the lost sheep and coin.

▶ Whom do you celebrate with when something good happens?

Pray

Turning from doing wrong to right is called *repentance*. Begin your prayer facing one direction. Tell God something you have done wrong. Then turn to face the other direction. Tell God how you will do things differently.

Peace Path
I Am Not Alone

Have you ever been lost? It can be scary! In Jesus' parable of the lost sheep and lost coin, the shepherd and woman never gave up looking for what they lost. Know that you will never be forgotten! God is always with you.

PAGE 330

Parable of a Family

LUKE 15:11-32

JESUS TOLD ANOTHER PARABLE:

"A man had two sons. The younger son said to him, 'Father, give me the money that I would get after you die.' The father gave it to him. The son took the money and went to a faraway country. There he quickly wasted all the money.

A great famine came, and the crops did not grow. The son did not have any food. He got a job feeding pigs. He was so hungry that he would have gladly eaten the pigs' food.

Finally, he came to his senses and said, 'My father's servants have lots of food, but here I am dying of hunger! I will go home and tell my father that I have sinned.'

The son went home. His father saw him and ran out to greet him. The father hugged and kissed his son. The son said, 'Father, I sinned against God and against you. I'm not good enough to be your son. Treat me like a servant.'

But his father said to the servants, 'Quick! Get the best clothes for my son! Give him a ring and sandals. Make a big meal so we can celebrate!'

The older son had been working in the field. When he came near the house, he heard music and saw people dancing. What was happening? A servant told him, 'Your brother has come home. Your father is having a special celebration for him.' The older son was very angry and refused to go inside.

The father came out, begging him to join the party. But the older son said, 'For years, I have been working for you every day. I never disobey you. I did not run away and waste your money like my brother did. But now you give him a party, and I get nothing.'

The father said, 'My son, you are always with me. Everything I have is yours. But we must celebrate! Your brother was dead and is now alive; he was lost and now he is found.'"

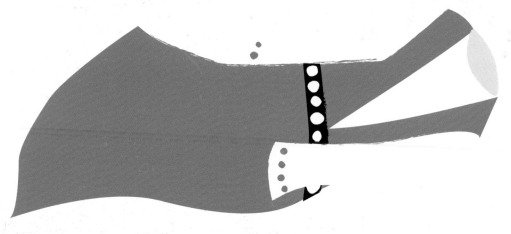

Wonder & Share 💡

▶ I wonder how the younger son felt when his father hugged him.

▶ What do you think happened next in the story?

Pray 💬

Use your body to express a joyful prayer celebrating something good that happened in

Peace Path 🕊️
Family Problems

The older brother was angry when it seemed like his father was treating him unfairly. What can you do or say when you feel like things are unfair in your family?

👉 This is the end of the path!
Go to **PAGE 16** to choose another

Where Is Your Treasure?

MATTHEW 19:16-30

ONE DAY, a young man came to Jesus and asked, "Teacher, what good thing must I do to have eternal life?"

Jesus replied, "Why do you ask me about what is good? Only God is good. If you want to enter into life, keep the commandments."

"Which ones?" the young man asked.

Jesus said, "Do not murder. Be faithful to your marriage. Do not steal. Do not lie about your neighbors. Honor and respect your parents. Also, you must love your neighbor as yourself."

The young man said, "I have kept all of these commandments; what else do I need to do?"

Jesus looked at him with love and said, "Go, sell the things you have, and give the money to people who are poor. Then you will have treasure in heaven and can come follow me."

This made the young man upset. He had lots of money and many fine things. He did not want to give them up. He went away sad.

Jesus turned to his disciples and told them, "It will be hard for a rich person to enter the kingdom of heaven. In fact, it is easier for a camel to go through the eye of a needle than it is for a rich person to enter God's kingdom."

Jesus' words shocked the disciples. They said, "Then who can be saved?"

Jesus gazed at them and said, "For people, it is impossible. Only through God are all things possible."

Peter was quick to reply, "Look, we have left everything and followed you. What will we get for this?"

Jesus answered, "One day, when all things are being made new, when I am seated on the throne in glory, all my followers will be with me. Everyone who has left houses, land, or had to turn away from family members will be blessed with something even greater: eternal life. In the world to come, those who are first will be last, and the last will be first."

Wonder & Share 💡

▶ I wonder how Jesus felt when the young man went away.

▶ Imagine "all things are being made new." What would you want God to make new in our world?

Pray 💬

Pray for people in your community who do not have enough food, clothing, or shelter.

Dig In 📖

Jesus named five commandments. Turn to page 62 to find the rest of the commandments that God gave to Moses on Mount Sinai.

Parable of the Vineyard Owner

MATTHEW 20:1-16

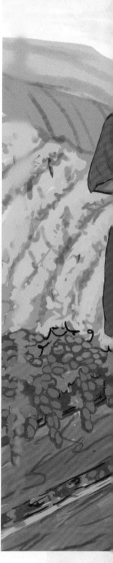

JESUS TOLD A PARABLE:

"God's kingdom is like a person who owned a vineyard. Early in the morning, the owner hired workers to pick the grapes. They agreed on a payment of one denarius for the day's work.

At nine o'clock, the owner of the vineyard went to the market and hired more workers. At noon and three o'clock, the owner went out again and hired more workers, each time promising a fair payment.

At five o'clock the owner noticed even more people in the market and said, 'Why are you standing here all day without working?'

'No one hired us,' they said. So the owner hired those workers too.

Later that evening, all the workers came to be paid. The owner began by paying the last people hired and then going to the first. Each worker got one denarius.

The people who had worked since early in the morning were angry when they too got just one denarius. They said, 'We worked longer than everyone else. We should get more money!'

But the owner said, 'I am being fair to you. You agreed to work for that amount of money. Are you upset because I give freely and generously to other people?'"

Wonder & Share 💡

▶ I wonder how the five o'clock workers felt when they saw how much money they received.

▶ How could you show extra kindness to someone today?

Pray 💬

The vineyard owner went out to find workers at different times of the day. Choose several times that you can pray today. You could use the morning and evening prayers on page 342.

Live It ☀

Learn about the people who grow and harvest food in your community and around the world. Write the name of each group of people on a sticky note and place it on your refrigerator as a reminder to pray and give thanks for their work.

Parable of the Sheep and Goats

MATTHEW 25:31–45

JESUS TOLD THE DISCIPLES A STORY:

"When the Son of Man comes, he will sit on a throne of glory as a great king. All nations will come before him. He will put them in two groups, like a shepherd separates the sheep from the goats. The sheep will be at his right, and the goats at his left.

The king will say to those on his right,
'God has blessed you and will give you the kingdom.
I was hungry and you gave me food.
I was thirsty and you gave me a drink.
I was a stranger and you welcomed me.
I needed clothes and you gave them to me.
I was sick and you cared for me.
I was in prison and you visited me.'
They will ask, 'When did we do those things for you?'
The king will answer, 'When you did them for the least of my people, you did them for me.'

Then the king will say to those on his left,
'God's kingdom will never be yours.
I was hungry and you did not give me food.
I was thirsty and you did not give me a drink.
I was a stranger and you did not welcome me.
I needed clothes and you did not give me any.
I was sick and you did not care for me.
I was in prison and you did not visit me.'
They will ask, 'When did we fail to do those things for you?'
The king will say, 'When you did not help the least of my people, you failed to help me. Eternal life is given to those who care for people who are overlooked or forgotten.'"

Wonder & Share 💡

▶ How are the children caring for each other in the story illustration?

▶ Share about a time you helped someone.

Pray 💬

Pray for one or more groups of people from the story (hungry, thirsty, a stranger, needing clothes, sick, in prison).

Peace Path

Love Your Neighbor

Look at the "Peace with Others" ideas on pages 352–353. Which ones are used in this Bible story? Choose one to do this week.

👉 **PAGE 298**

Lazarus, Come Out!

JOHN 11:1-44

WINTER CAME. Jesus went to Jerusalem for the Festival of the Dedication. Some of the leaders there tried to arrest him. He escaped with his disciples and went to a small town across the Jordan River.

A message came from his friends Mary and Martha who lived in Bethany. Their brother Lazarus was very sick. Could Jesus come and help?

Jesus loved them very much. Yet he waited two more days before going to their home. By that time, Lazarus had been dead for four days. Martha and Mary's friends came to comfort them.

When Martha heard that Jesus was coming, she hurried out to meet him. "If you had come sooner, my brother would not have died," she said. "But even still, I know that God will give you whatever you ask."

Jesus said, "Lazarus will live again. I am the resurrection and the life. Anyone who believes in me will never die. Do you believe this?"

Martha said, "I believe that you are the Messiah, the Son of God, the one who has come to save us."

Martha went back home and told Mary, "The Teacher is calling for you."

Mary ran out to greet Jesus. Her friends followed. She knelt at his feet, weeping. Through her tears she said, "If you had been here, my brother would not have died." Jesus saw her tears and was deeply moved. He began to cry too.

Then Jesus, the sisters, and their friends went to the tomb. "Take away the stone in front of the tomb," Jesus said. But Martha said, "He has been dead for four days! It already smells bad."

"Do you not remember my words?" Jesus asked. "If you believe, you will see the glory of God."

So they took away the stone. Jesus looked up and prayed, "Thank you, God, for hearing me!" Then he called out with a loud voice, "Lazarus, come out!" Lazarus did! His hands, feet, and face were wrapped with strips of cloth. Jesus said, "Remove the cloth and let him go."

Wonder & Share ☀

▶ I wonder how the sisters felt as they waited for Jesus to come.

▶ Tell about a time you cried with someone. Who comforts you when you feel sad?

Pray 💬

At the beginning and end of your prayer, repeat the words of Jesus' prayer: "Thank you, God, for hearing me."

Peace Path 🖐

God Is Amazing

It seems impossible that a person could be raised from the dead! Yet, that is exactly what happened to Lazarus. He is not the only one in the Bible who was brought back to life. Follow this peace path to discover another resurrection story.

 PAGE 282

Let the Children Come

MARK 10:13–16

JESUS AND HIS DISCIPLES went into the region of Judea and across the Jordan River. Again, crowds of people followed him, and he stopped to teach them.

People began bringing children toward Jesus so he could bless them. But the disciples said, "Go away. Stop bothering Jesus."

When Jesus heard the disciples' mean words, he felt very angry. He called to them with a loud voice, "Let the little children come to me! Do not ever stop them. God's kingdom belongs to those who are like these children. Do you want to enter God's kingdom? Then you must receive it like a child."

The disciples stepped aside, and the children gathered around Jesus. Jesus took them in his arms, laid his hands on them, and blessed them. And no one was forgotten.

Wonder & Share

▶ I wonder why the disciples did not want the children near Jesus.

▶ Imagine the children coming to Jesus. I wonder where they came from and how they looked.

▶ Jesus spoke up to protect children. Who else works to keep people safe?

Pray

Say a prayer of blessing for children.

Peace Path

I Am Special

Jesus made each child feel safe, loved, and important. Who helps you feel that way? Maybe it feels like no one cares about you or someone has even hurt you. Imagine Jesus saying a blessing just for you. Then read the words on page 351 aloud several times.

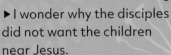 **PAGE 316**

Bartimaeus

MARK 10:46-52

ON THE WAY TO JERUSALEM, Jesus and his disciples approached Jericho, a city in the Jordan Valley. As usual, a large crowd followed them.

Bartimaeus sat along the dusty road outside the city. He was blind and could not work, so he had to beg for money to buy food. Bartimaeus heard people's footsteps as they passed by, yet no one gave him any money. Did they even look at him, Bartimaeus wondered? Did they see that he needed help?

Then Bartimaeus heard the news: Jesus of Nazareth was coming down the road, right toward where he was sitting. Surely Jesus would help him. As Jesus and the crowd drew near, Bartimaeus began to shout, "Jesus, Son of David, have mercy on me!"

"Be quiet!" a man in the crowd said to him angrily.

"Stop shouting!" said another. "Leave Jesus alone."

But Bartimaeus shouted even louder, "Jesus, Son of David, have mercy on me!"

Jesus stopped a short distance from Bartimaeus and said, "Call him here."

Bartimaeus threw off his coat, jumped up, and came to Jesus. Jesus asked, "What do you want me to do for you?"

Bartimaeus said, "Teacher, I want to see again!"

Jesus said, "Go, your faith has healed you." Right away, Bartimaeus was able to see. He followed Jesus.

Wonder & Share

▶ I wonder why people in the crowd tried to stop Bartimaeus from talking to Jesus.

▶ Sometimes people ask for help again and again, but no one listens or does anything. Talk about how it feels to be ignored or left on your own.

Pray 💬

Bartimaeus asked Jesus for help. What do you want Jesus to do for you? Tell God in words or draw a picture to show your prayer.

Dig In 📖

Jesus told a parable that took place on the road between Jerusalem and Jericho, the very road that Jesus was traveling when he met Bartimaeus. Read the parable on page 230.

Zacchaeus

LUKE 19:1-10

AFTER HEALING BARTIMAEUS, Jesus went into Jericho. Zacchaeus, the chief tax collector, lived there. He was rich and had fancy clothes and a fine home. But he did not have many friends. His neighbors hated him. He worked for the Roman government and cheated the people in his own city, demanding more money than was required by the law and keeping it for himself.

Zacchaeus heard that Jesus was coming. Zacchaeus wanted to see Jesus, but he was a short man and knew he wouldn't be able to see over the crowd. So he ran ahead and climbed into a sycamore tree along the road.

When Jesus came to the tree, he looked up and said, "Zacchaeus, hurry and come down! I am going to stay at your home today."

Zacchaeus quickly climbed down. He was happy to welcome Jesus into his home. What a special honor!

All the people grumbled to each other, "Zacchaeus is a sinner and treats us harshly. Why would Jesus go to his house?"

Zacchaeus heard them and stopped. Turning to Jesus, he said, "I will give half of what I own to people who are poor. For each person I have cheated, I will pay back four times what I took."

Jesus said, "Salvation is here today! Zacchaeus is part of the family of God. I have come to find and save those who are lost."

Wonder & Share

▶ I wonder why Jesus decided to go to Zacchaeus' house.
▶ Zacchaeus had a plan for making things right with the people he had treated unfairly. Make a plan for what to do if you hurt someone.

Pray 💬

Use the prayer path on page 346. Follow the prayer instructions as you move your finger through the neighborhood.

Peace Path

God Welcomes All

People were upset that Jesus would be friends with Zacchaeus, who had done many wrong and hurtful things. Jesus reminded them that Zacchaeus was still part of God's family, despite what he had done. Zacchaeus could make things right.

PAGE 300

Mary's Gift

JOHN 12:1-8

THE TEMPLE LEADERS found out that Jesus had raised Lazarus from the dead and that he continued to heal many people. If they did not stop Jesus, more and more people would believe in him. The leaders ordered people to report where Jesus was so they could arrest him.

After that, Jesus had to be careful where he went. He stayed in a town near the wilderness until six days before the Passover festival. Then Jesus went to the town of Bethany, where Mary and Martha lived with their brother Lazarus.

They had a special dinner for Jesus. The friends ate the delicious food that Martha prepared. They talked and laughed together. Jesus told them stories of his travels and the people he met.

During the meal, Mary slipped out of the room to get a special gift she had bought for Jesus. It was a jar of expensive perfume made from nard. Kneeling in front of Jesus, she poured the perfume on his feet and wiped them with her hair. The beautiful smell of the perfume filled the house.

Judas, the disciple who was making plans to betray Jesus, said, "Why did she waste this perfume? It was worth a year's pay. She could have sold it and given the money to people who are poor." (Judas did not actually care about people who were poor. He was in charge of the group's money and sometimes stole some.)

But Jesus said, "Leave Mary alone. She bought the perfume for the day of my burial and has anointed me now. There will always be people who need money, but you do not always have me."

Wonder & Share

▶ I wonder how Jesus felt while Mary was anointing his feet.
▶ When did you get a gift for someone and couldn't wait to give it to them?

Pray 💬

Find something that has a beautiful smell, such as a flower, spice, perfume, or lotion. Breathe deeply of the sweet smell as you pray.

Dig In 📖

The perfume was made from *spikenard,* a flowering plant that grows in the Himalayas, a mountain range in India, China, and Nepal.

Hosanna!

MARK 11:1-11; LUKE 19:28-40

JESUS AND HIS DISCIPLES were on their way to Jerusalem for the Passover festival. As they came near the Mount of Olives, Jesus sent two of them to the next town and said, "You will find the colt of a donkey there that has never been ridden. Untie it and bring it to me. Tell anyone who asks that the Lord needs it and will send it back soon."

The two disciples went into town, searching for a colt. They saw sheep and goats and chickens, but no donkeys. There were horses and cows, but no donkeys. Finally, they found a colt on a side street, tied near a door. As they untied it, the people standing nearby protested, "What are you doing? You can't just take the colt!"

The two disciples said, "The Lord needs it and will send it back soon." The people agreed to let them take the colt.

Bringing the colt to Jesus, the disciples laid their cloaks on its back. Jesus rode it toward Jerusalem.

A great crowd of people gathered around him. Some spread their cloaks on the road in front of Jesus. Some cut leafy branches from the nearby fields and laid them on the road.

The crowd began to praise God for all the amazing things they had seen. They shouted,

"**Hosanna!**
Blessed is the king who comes in the name of the Lord!
Peace in heaven. Glory to God!
Hosanna in the highest heaven!"

But some Pharisees in the crowd said to Jesus, "Teacher, tell the people to stop shouting."

Jesus said, "If they are quiet, the stones will shout!"

Wonder & Share

▶ I wonder why Jesus wanted to ride on a donkey colt.
▶ If Jesus came to your community, how would you celebrate?

Pray

Find a leafy branch to wave as you read the blessing of the crowd (*bold print in the story*) as your prayer. Or cut a leaf shape from paper to wave.

Dig In

"Blessed is the one who comes in the name of the Lord" is from Psalm 118:26 and is sung at the three Jewish pilgrimage festivals: Pesach (*Passover*), Shavuot (*Feast of Weeks*), and Sukkot (*Festival of Booths*).

Turning the Tables

MARK 11:15–19

UPON ARRIVING IN JERUSALEM, Jesus and his disciples went into the temple. People from many lands had arrived for the Passover festival and had come to worship at the temple.

Money changers called out, "You must make a payment to the temple. Give me the money from your homeland, and I will exchange it for the silver coin you need."

Sellers shouted over the noise of the crowd, "Come and buy my sheep and doves for your offering."

It did not look or sound like a holy place for worshiping God. It was more like a busy market.

Jesus felt very angry! He flipped over the tables of the money changers, scattering their coins. He overturned the chairs of the people selling animals. He refused to let anyone carry things through the temple.

When the coins stopped rolling and the animals and people had quieted, Jesus reminded them of the words of the prophets Isaiah and Jeremiah:

> "My house is to be a house of prayer
>   for all peoples.
> But you have made it into a den for robbers!"

When the chief priests and scribes heard about what Jesus had done, they kept looking for a way to kill him. But they were afraid of him since the crowds were so amazed by everything Jesus said and did.

Wonder & Share ☀

▶ I wonder what a house of prayer for all people would look and sound like?

▶ Jesus felt angry when he saw what was happening in the temple. What wrong things make you feel angry?

Pray 💬

The temple was to be a house of prayer for everyone. Create a special place to pray in your home. Gather there as a family and give each person time to pray.

Dig In 📖

Look at the diagram of the temple on page 367. Find the Gentiles' Courtyard, also called the Outer Court, where this story probably took place. This area was open to all people, including people from other lands who were not Jewish.

The Greatest Commandment

MARK 12:28–34

ANOTHER DAY when Jesus was in the temple, a scribe came to him. The scribe had overheard Jesus arguing with other leaders about difficult questions. The scribe knew all the laws and commandments that people in the temple were supposed to follow. He had his own question: "Which commandment is the most important of all?"

Jesus said, "The first is, 'Hear O Israel: The Lord our God, the Lord is one; you shall love the Lord your God with all your heart, soul, mind, and strength.' The second is this: 'You shall love your neighbor as yourself.' Nothing is more important than these."

The scribe said, "Teacher, this is right. Loving God wholeheartedly and loving your neighbor as yourself—these things are more important than all the offerings and sacrifices we can give."

Jesus saw the man's wisdom and said, "You are close to God's kingdom."

No one dared to ask Jesus any more questions after that.

Wonder & Share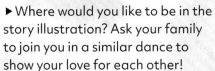

▶ Where would you like to be in the story illustration? Ask your family to join you in a similar dance to show your love for each other!

▶ How can you love God with your whole self? Look at the "Peace with God" ideas on pages 348–349.

Pray 💬

Choose motions for these words: *love, heart, soul, mind, strength*. Use your motions as you say this prayer: "God, help me to **love** you with all my **heart**, all my **soul,** all my **mind**, and all my **strength**. Amen."

Live It ☀

Make a list of five things you can do to love your neighbors. Post the list where you'll see it regularly. Do one thing each week until you've completed the list.

A Generous Offering

MARK 12:38-44

JESUS CONTINUED TEACHING in the temple. The crowd listened in with delight. They loved hearing what Jesus had to say.

Jesus warned them, "Watch out for the scribes. They like to walk around wearing long, fancy robes. They want to be greeted with honor in the market. They choose the very best seats in the synagogue and the most important places at banquets. They cheat widows out of their homes and say long prayers to get everyone's attention. They will be judged for what they do."

Jesus and his disciples then sat near the place where people gave their offerings. Many people who were rich gave lots of money. A widow who was very poor stepped forward and put in two small copper coins worth one penny.

Jesus said to his disciples, "This woman gave more than everyone else." What did Jesus mean? The disciples had seen how much more money the other people gave. Jesus went on, "Everyone's gifts are important. But the rich people gave the extra money they did not need, while the widow gave everything she had to live on."

Wonder & Share

▶ I wonder what happened to the woman after she gave away all her money.
▶ What can you offer to God other than money? Think of your skills and interests. How could you use them to love God or your neighbor?

Pray

Jesus told the crowd that it was not important to say long prayers to impress other people. Turn to page 344 and choose a short breath prayer to repeat several times.

Live It ☀

Choose a place or organization to give a gift of money, no matter how small. What good things are they doing in the world?

A Gift to Remember

MARK 14:3-9

IT WAS TWO DAYS before the Passover festival. Jesus was having dinner at the home of his friend Simon. Many people avoided Simon because he had leprosy, a skin disease. They did not want to get leprosy too.

During dinner, a woman came in with a jar of very expensive perfume made from nard. She poured the perfume on Jesus' head to anoint him, just as kings were anointed. The smell of the perfume filled the house.

Some of the disciples were angry and said mean things to the woman. Why did she waste the perfume? It could have been sold for lots of money, and the money given to people who were poor.

But Jesus said, "Leave her alone. Why are you speaking to her this way? She showed great love to me. There will always be people among you who need money, and you can be kind to them whenever you want. But I will not always be here. She anointed me before my death and burial. Whenever the good news is told in the whole world, what she has done will also be told in memory of her."

Wonder & Share

▶ I wonder who the woman was.

▶ I wonder what good news Jesus was talking about.

Pray 💬

Follow the prayer path on page 347. As you move toward the middle of the path, think of a time someone was mean to you. Pause in the middle of the path. Imagine Jesus comforting and protecting you as you move back to the start.

Practice Peace 🕊

What can you do when someone says mean things to you or a friend?

Jesus Washes Feet

JOHN 13:1-15

JESUS KNEW that he was going to die while he was in Jerusalem. As he thought about leaving this world, he was reminded how much he loved his disciples. He would love them until the very end.

So that night during dinner with his disciples, Jesus got up from the table. He took off his outer robe and tied a towel around his waist. He poured water into a basin and began to wash his disciples' feet, drying them with the towel. The disciples looked back and forth. Why was he doing this? This was a servant's job.

Jesus knelt before Simon Peter, who said, "Lord, are you really going to wash my feet?"

Jesus nodded, saying, "Right now you don't understand what I am doing, but later you will."

Peter resisted. "You will never wash my feet," he said.

"I must wash your feet for you to belong to me," Jesus replied.

Now Peter understood. "Then wash my feet and hands and head!" he said eagerly.

But Jesus said, "A person who has bathed does not need to be washed again, except for the feet. You are clean, although not everyone at this table is." Jesus said this because he knew that Judas was going to betray him.

After washing everyone's feet, he put on his robe and came back to the table. "Do you understand what I have done?" Jesus asked. "You call me Teacher and Lord, and you are right. That is what I am. I have set an example for you as your teacher. I have washed your feet. Now do as I have done and wash each other's feet."

Wonder & Share 💡
▶ I wonder what it means to belong to Jesus.
▶ Jesus set an example for his disciples, who were learning from him. How could you set a positive example for someone younger than you?

Pray 💬
Jesus loved his disciples very much. Pray for people you love.

Live It ☀
Follow Jesus' example and wash a friend's or a family member's feet! How did you each feel?

Peace I Leave with You

JOHN 13:33–15:19

AFTER JESUS WASHED HIS DISCIPLES' FEET and they finished dinner, Jesus said to them, "I will only be with you a little longer. Love one another, just like I have loved you. People will know you are my disciples if you love each other. Don't let your heart be troubled or worried. I am going to prepare a place for you with God. You know the way to the place I am going."

Thomas said, "We don't know where you are going. How can we know the way?"

Jesus said, "I am the way, the truth, and the life. By knowing me, you know God. After I leave, God will send the Spirit to comfort you and be with you forever. The Spirit will teach you and remind you of all I've said. Peace I leave with you; my peace I give to you. You do not need to be afraid."

Jesus went on, "God is the vine-grower and I am the vine. You are the branches. A branch cannot bear fruit if it is separated from the vine. In the same way, when you remain connected to me, you will grow and bear fruit.

Rest in the great love I have for you. Let it bring joy to your hearts. Love one another just as I have loved you. You are not my servants; you are my friends. I shared everything I have heard from God with you. Other people may hate you, but I chose you and I love you."

Wonder & Share

▶ I wonder how God's Spirit comforts us.
▶ What helps us stay connected to Jesus?
▶ Share about a time you felt worried and a time you felt at peace.

Pray

Turn to page 344 and create your own breath prayer. Choose a name for God and then a simple prayer related to the Bible story like "give me peace," "comfort me," or "be with me."

Peace Path
I Need Comfort

Which words of Jesus from this story are most comforting to you? Next time you feel sad or worried, try one of the "Peace Inside" ideas on page 350.

 PAGE 322

The Last Supper

MATTHEW 26:1–5, 14–30;
MARK 14:12–26; LUKE 22:1–23

IT WAS TIME FOR PASSOVER, the seven-day festival when Jews remembered God freeing them from slavery in Egypt. Judas, one of Jesus' disciples, snuck away to plan with the leaders and temple police how to arrest Jesus.

"What will you give me if I betray Jesus to you?" Judas asked them. They offered him 30 pieces of silver, and Judas took the money. He began looking for an opportunity to turn Jesus over to them.

On the first day of Passover, Jesus gave Peter and John instructions to prepare for the holy Passover meal: "When you enter the city, you will find a man carrying a jar of water. Follow him and go to the house he enters. In that house, ask for a guest room for your teacher to eat Passover." They followed Jesus' words, and everything happened just as he said.

That night as they all gathered at the Passover table, Jesus told his disciples, "I have longed to eat this Passover meal with you before I suffer."

Then he took a loaf of bread, thanked God for it, broke it, and gave it to them, saying, "This bread is my body, which is given for you. Eat this to remember me."

He took a cup, and after giving thanks, he shared it with them and said, "This is my blood, which will be poured out for many. When I die, there will be a new covenant between God and all people."

After this Jesus warned them, "Someone here at this table is going to betray me." The disciples were worried and confused. Who would do that? (Jesus was speaking about Judas.)

Jesus and the disciples sang a hymn together, and then they went out to the Mount of Olives.

Wonder & Share 💡
▶ I wonder why Judas decided to betray Jesus.
▶ Tell about a special meal you have shared with people you love.

Pray 💬
Choose a meal prayer from page 344 to say the next time you eat.

Live It ☀
Eating the bread and drinking the cup is one way to remember Jesus. How else can you remember Jesus this week?

Jesus Suffers

COMPILED FROM THE GOSPELS OF MATTHEW, MARK, LUKE, AND JOHN

AFTER THE PASSOVER MEAL, Jesus and his disciples went to the garden called Gethsemane. Jesus knelt and prayed, "Father, I do not want to suffer or be killed. But I want your will to be done."

A large crowd came with swords and torches. Judas, one of Jesus' disciples, led them. He went right to Jesus and kissed him on the cheek, showing the soldiers whom to arrest. Another disciple asked Jesus, "Should we fight them with our swords?"

No, Jesus did not want that.

The soldiers in the crowd arrested Jesus and took him to the high priest's house. Jesus' disciple Peter followed. He wanted to help Jesus, but instead Peter denied that he even knew Jesus.

Many people told lies about Jesus to the high priest, but Jesus stayed silent. He did not defend himself. The high priest asked, "Are you the Son of God?"

"I am," said Jesus. This was all the leaders needed to hear. They agreed Jesus must be put to death.

Early in the morning, the Jewish leaders took Jesus to Pilate, the Roman governor. Pilate asked Jesus many questions, then called together the chief priests, leaders, and the people. He said to them, "Jesus has not broken any laws. He is innocent. I am going to let him go."

But the crowd became angry and shouted at Pilate to have Jesus killed. So Pilate handed Jesus over to his soldiers. They put a purple robe and crown of thorns on Jesus, whipped him, and sent him away with the crowd to die.

Simon of Cyrene carried Jesus' cross for him until they reached Golgotha, the Place of the Skull. Women wept for Jesus on the way.

As the soldiers put him on the cross, Jesus prayed, "Father, forgive them. They do not know what they are doing."

Some people passed by and said mean things to Jesus. But many people who loved him were also there: his mother, his aunt, Mary the wife of Clopas, and Mary Magdalene stood right near the cross. John his disciple was there too. Other women who had followed Jesus stood at a distance. He was not alone in his pain.

For three hours in the middle of the day, the sky turned dark. Then, crying out in a loud voice, Jesus said, "Father, my life is in your hands." He bowed his head and died.

Seeing this, a Roman soldier said, "This man really was the Son of God."

Joseph of Arimathea took Jesus' body down from the cross. He and Nicodemus wrapped Jesus' body in strips of linen cloth and spices and laid it in a new tomb. They put a large stone in the entrance of the tomb.

Mary Magdalene and Mary watched, then hurried home to prepare more spices. It was Friday afternoon and the Sabbath rest would soon begin. For Jesus' followers, all hope seemed lost.

Wonder & Share

▶ How does this story make you feel?

▶ How did people show love for Jesus during this awful time?

▶ What can you do when you see someone who is sad, lonely, scared, or in pain?

Pray 💬

This is a hard and painful story. Choose from the "Ways to Pray" on pages 340–341 and then say a prayer of *lament*. This means talking to God about a terrible thing that has happened. In lament, we share our hard questions and feelings with God.

Dig In 📖

When Jesus died on the cross, he made peace between us and God. By his death, Jesus broke down the walls of hatred that divide us so that we can be one people. Read more about it in Ephesians 2 on page 320.

He Is Risen!

MARK 16:1-8; LUKE 24:1-12

IT WAS THE FIRST DAY OF THE WEEK. The sun rose, brushing away the darkness of night. Mary Magdalene, Joanna, and James' mother Mary were on their way to Jesus' tomb. They carried the spices they had prepared for Jesus' body. As they came near the tomb, Mary said in surprise, "Look! The stone has been rolled away from the tomb!"

"How can this be?" wondered Joanna.

They looked inside the tomb. It was empty! Where was Jesus' body?

Suddenly two men in dazzling clothes stood before them. The women were terrified and bowed down with their faces on the ground. But the men said, "Why are you looking for the living here with the dead? Jesus has risen! He is no longer in the tomb! Remember how Jesus told you that he would die and rise again on the third day?"

The women did remember and hurried away to tell the news to the other disciples.

But one disciple said, "This is nonsense. Your story cannot be true."

"I saw Jesus die," said another. "He could not be alive again."

But Peter got up and ran to the tomb. Looking inside, he saw only the linen cloths. Jesus' body was not there! He went home, amazed by what he had seen.

Wonder & Share 💡

▶ I wonder where Jesus was.

▶ I wonder how the women felt when the other disciples did not believe what they said.

▶ What questions do you have about this story?

Pray 💬

Jesus is risen! Celebrate Jesus' resurrection with a joyful prayer of praise. Wave streamers, ribbons, or colorful cloths. Or dance to your favorite song.

Dig In 📖

Each Gospel has different details about Jesus' resurrection. In Matthew, there is an earthquake, and Jesus appears to the women as they leave the tomb. In Mark, the women run away, too afraid to tell anyone what they saw. Read John's version on the next page.

The Empty Tomb

JOHN 20:1-18

IT WAS THE FIRST DAY of the week. Early in the morning, while it was still dark, Mary Magdalene went to Jesus' tomb. The stone had been rolled away from the entrance to the tomb!

She ran to tell Peter and John. "They have taken Jesus from the tomb," she exclaimed. "I don't know where they put him!"

Peter and John raced each other to the tomb. John got there first and bent to look inside. All he saw were the linen cloths that had been used to wrap Jesus' body. Peter came right behind him and went inside. Mary was right; Jesus' body was gone.

The two men went home, but Mary stood outside the tomb, weeping. She looked inside again and saw two angels in white sitting where Jesus' body had been. "Why are you crying?" they asked.

Mary said, "They have taken Jesus away. I do not know where he is." She turned and saw a man standing there. He said to her, "Woman, why are you crying? Who are you looking for?"

Mary thought the man was the gardener, so she pleaded, "If you have taken Jesus away, tell me where he is so that I can care for his body."

The man said, "Mary!" It was Jesus!

Mary turned and reached for him, crying out, "Teacher!"

Jesus said, "Go tell my disciples that I am going to be with my God and your God."

So Mary hurried off and told the disciples, "I have seen Jesus!" She told them everything Jesus said to her.

Wonder & Share

▶ I wonder why Mary did not recognize Jesus at first.

▶ Whom could you tell about the good news of Jesus' resurrection from the dead?

Pray

Like Mary, start your prayer by saying, "Teacher!"

Peace Path

God Is Amazing

After his death on the cross, Jesus was raised to life by the power of God. Jesus' resurrection is celebrated every year on Easter Sunday.

This is the end of the path! Go to **PAGE 16** to choose another peace path.

A Stranger on the Road

LUKE 24:13-35

LATER, on the day that Jesus rose from the dead, two of his disciples were walking from Jerusalem to Emmaus. One was named Cleopas. The two disciples were talking about the death of Jesus.

A man came and walked with them, wanting to know what they were talking about. Cleopas and his friend stopped, looking sad. They asked, "Are you the only person in Jerusalem who does not know what has happened?"

"What do you mean?" the man asked.

They replied, "Jesus of Nazareth was a prophet who did amazing things. We hoped that he would be our Messiah, the one to save us. But our priests and leaders turned him over to Pilate and he was killed. Now it is the third day, and we do not know where he is. Women from our group went to the tomb, but Jesus' body was not there. They had visions of angels who said he was alive."

The man said, "Wasn't it necessary for the Messiah to suffer and then return to glory?" He then reminded them of all that Moses and the prophets had said about the coming Messiah.

The men arrived in Emmaus and urged the traveler to stay with them since it was late in the day. While they were at dinner, the man took bread, blessed it, broke it, and then gave it to them. Suddenly, their eyes were opened, and they realized it was Jesus! Immediately Jesus disappeared.

Cleopas said to his friend, "Weren't our hearts burning within us as Jesus was talking to us on the road?"

They ran back to Jerusalem and told the disciples, "Jesus has risen! We met him on the road, and he broke bread for us."

Wonder & Share

▶ I wonder why Jesus did not tell the disciples who he was right away.

▶ What feelings do you think the two men had throughout the story? Share about times you had those same feelings.

Pray 💬

The friends were traveling from one city to another. Choose a "road" to follow on the prayer path on page 346. Complete the prayer prompts along the way.

Dig In 📖

The men only knew it was Jesus when he broke bread and gave it to them. Look at page 274 to see another time Jesus broke bread and gave it to his disciples.

My Lord and My God!

JOHN 20:19-31

THAT EVENING, after Jesus rose from the dead, the disciples were gathered in a locked room. They were afraid of the leaders who had put Jesus to death. Suddenly Jesus stood among them and said, "Peace be with you." He showed them the wounds on his hands and side from when he had died. They were filled with joy to see him alive.

Again Jesus said, "Peace be with you. Just as God sent me into the world, I am sending you." He breathed on them, saying, "Receive the Holy Spirit."

Thomas, one of Jesus' disciples, was not with them that night. The disciples later told him about seeing Jesus. But Thomas said, "I will not believe unless I touch his hands and his side."

Eight days later, the disciples were again in the locked room, and Thomas was with them. Even though the doors were locked, Jesus suddenly stood among them and said, "Peace be with you."

He turned to Thomas and said, "Touch my hands and my side. Do not doubt but believe!"

Thomas said to Jesus, "My Lord and my God!"

Jesus replied, "You believed because you saw me. Blessed are those who believe even if they do not see me."

Jesus did many more amazing signs that are not written in this book. But these are written so that you will believe that Jesus is the Son of God. When you believe in him, you will have new life!

Wonder & Share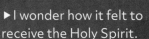

▶ I wonder how it felt to receive the Holy Spirit.

▶ I wonder what other amazing things Jesus did that weren't written down.

Pray 💬

Create a breath prayer from page 344. Choose a name for God from the list and then say, "give me peace." Repeat this several times.

Live It ☀

We are not able to see Jesus, but we can still trust and believe in him! Turn to pages 348–349 to discover other ways to experience peace with God.

Breakfast on the Beach

JOHN 21:1-14

IT HAD BEEN A LONG NIGHT for the disciples. Peter, Thomas, Nathanael, James, John, and two other disciples had gone out to fish on the Sea of Galilee. Again and again, they cast their nets into the water. Again and again, they came up empty—a whole night's work and nothing to show for it.

The sun rose bright the next morning. The disciples looked across the water and saw a man standing on the shore. The man called out, "Children, you did not catch any fish; did you?"

"No," they replied.

"Cast your net on the right side of the boat, and you will catch some," he told them.

Again? Throw the net again? They had done this all night. But perhaps it was worth one more try. The disciples cast their net on the right side. Fish swarmed the net. The disciples could not even haul the net back into the boat because there were so many fish!

John exclaimed to Peter, "It is Jesus!"

Peter was so excited he jumped into the water and waded toward shore. The other disciples came in the boat, dragging the net of fish.

When they came ashore, the disciples saw a charcoal fire with fish cooking on it. There were loaves of bread too. Jesus said, "Bring some of the fish you caught."

Peter and the others hauled the net onto the beach. It was full of large fish—153 in all!

"Come and have breakfast," Jesus said, offering them bread and fish to eat.

This was the third time that Jesus appeared to the disciples after being raised from the dead.

Wonder & Share 💡

▶ I wonder how the disciples felt when they worked all night but did not catch any fish.

▶ Share about a time you ate outside. Or go have your first outdoor meal! What do you like about eating outside?

Pray 💬

Choose a meal prayer from page 344 and say it at breakfast.

Live It ☀️

Make a special breakfast. Tell stories about times you worked together with others. Did everything go as planned?

To Heaven and the Ends of the Earth

ACTS 1:1–11

FOR 40 DAYS after Jesus rose from the dead, he met with his disciples and continued to teach them about God's kingdom.

He told them, "Don't leave Jerusalem yet. God will soon give you the Holy Spirit. John baptized you with water, but God will baptize you with the Holy Spirit."

The disciples asked, "Are you going to bring back the kingdom of Israel?"

Jesus said, "Do not worry about dates and times. God knows what is best. But you will be filled with power when the Holy Spirit comes. Then you will tell everyone about me—here in Jerusalem, in the nearby towns and villages, in faraway countries, even to the ends of the earth. You will share the good news with all people everywhere!"

Just then, Jesus was taken up into a cloud. The disciples could not see him anymore and kept staring at the great expanse of sky.

Suddenly two men in white robes appeared. "Why are you looking up into the sky?" they asked. "Jesus went to heaven but will come again in the same way you saw him go."

After Jesus went to heaven, his disciples were called apostles. The apostles went back to Jerusalem. They prayed together as they waited for the coming of the Holy Spirit.

Wonder & Share

▶ I wonder how each person in the story illustration is feeling.
▶ The believers had to wait for the coming of the Holy Spirit. When have you had to wait for something exciting to happen?

Pray 💬

Use the prayer path on page 346 as you pray. Be sure to stop at the airport so you can pray for people around the world!

Live It ☀

Jesus told his disciples to speak about him at home, in nearby places, and far away. Whom could you talk to about Jesus? What might you say?

A New Apostle

ACTS 1:12-26

AFTER JESUS RETURNED TO HEAVEN, the apostles went back to Jerusalem and gathered in the upstairs room where they had been staying. Peter, Andrew, James, John, Philip, Thomas, Bartholomew, Matthew, James, Simon, and Judas son of James were there. They spent their time praying with Jesus' mother and brothers, as well as several women who had followed Jesus. Only Judas Iscariot—the one who had betrayed Jesus—was not with them.

One day, a crowd of 120 believers came together. Peter stood up and said, "Friends, the scriptures told us that someone would betray Jesus. It was Judas, and he has now died. The scriptures also say that we must choose another person to take his position as leader. It must be someone who has followed Jesus from the very beginning—from the time of John the Baptist—and continued until Jesus went back to heaven."

Two men who had been faithful followers of Jesus were brought forward: Joseph, called Barsabbas, and Matthias. The apostles prayed, "God, you know the heart of every person. Show us which one of these men you have chosen to take the place of Judas and be a witness throughout the world."

They cast lots and Matthias was chosen. He was added as an apostle to Jesus' other 11 apostles.

Wonder & Share 💡

▶ I wonder how Matthias and Barsabbas felt as the apostles were praying for them.

▶ The disciples prayed as a group. Would you rather pray alone or with a group? Why?

Pray 💬

The believers prayed to help them make an important decision. Ask for God's help to decide something in your life.

Dig In 📖

Casting lots was one way to seek God's will and make important decisions. Often stones or sticks were marked to show the possible options, and then one was chosen at random. When Jesus died, soldiers cast lots to decide who would get his clothes.

Pentecost

ACTS 2:1-39

IT WAS THE DAY OF PENTECOST. Many believers had gathered in a house in Jerusalem. Suddenly, a sound like a great rushing wind from heaven came down. The wind filled the whole house where the people were sitting. Little flames of fire appeared and danced on the head of each person in the house! All the people were filled with the Holy Spirit and began to speak in other languages.

Many faithful Jews from different countries were living in Jerusalem. When they heard all the noise, they gathered in curiosity. Each one heard the people in the home speaking a different language. They couldn't believe what they heard. The people said, "These people are from Galilee, but we are from more than 16 different countries. How can we hear them speaking in our own language?" Amazed, they wondered together, "What does this mean?"

Peter stood and said to the crowd, "Listen to the promises God made through the prophet Joel long ago:

'I will pour out my Spirit on all people.
　　Your children will speak my words.
Young people will see visions.
　　Old people will dream dreams.
I will pour out my Spirit on enslaved people;
　　they too will share my message.
Everyone who calls on God's name will be saved.'

Friends, God sent Jesus into the world. Jesus did amazing wonders and signs but was put to death on a cross. Yet God raised him up. Surely, he is the Messiah, the one who will save us."

The people felt deep sadness in their hearts about Jesus' death. They asked the apostles, "What should we do?" Peter replied, "Be baptized in the name of Jesus Christ. Then God will forgive your wrongs, and you will receive the gift of the Holy Spirit. This promise is for you, for your children, and for all who are far away. This is good news, for the Lord our God calls everyone."

Wonder & Share ☼
▶ Imagine so many different languages being spoken at once.
▶ God calls everyone. Name 10 people—some who live close and some who are far away. Say, "God calls _____ (*person's name*)."

Pray 💬
Light a candle as you pray to remember the flames of fire at Pentecost. After you pray, blow it out, remembering the great wind that came down.

Peace Path 🛐
God's Spirit Moves
What amazing things happened when God's Spirit came at Pentecost? Imagine God pouring out the Spirit on you!

🐍 This is the end of the path! Go to **PAGE 16** to choose another peace path.

Life Together

ACTS 2:41–47; ACTS 4:32–37

ON THE DAY THE HOLY SPIRIT CAME with wind and fire, about 3,000 people were baptized and became part of the group of believers. They were amazed by the signs and wonders that the apostles were doing. With great power, the apostles continued to teach them about the resurrection of Jesus.

Daily, the people spent time in the temple together—praising God, praying, and listening to the apostles teach. They joyfully ate meals together in their homes. They remembered Jesus by breaking bread and sharing wine, just as Jesus had done with his disciples.

The believers were one in heart and soul. They held everything in common. No one said, "This is mine." Instead, they shared everything. When someone was in need, the believers sold what they had—even their houses and land—and brought the money to the apostles. Then the apostles divided the money so that everyone had enough.

Barnabas, a Levite from Cyprus, was one of many people who shared what he had. He sold his field, then brought all the money and laid it at the apostles' feet.

Every day more and more people joined the group of believers.

Wonder & Share

▸ I wonder what the children shared with each other.
▸ The name *Barnabas* means "son of encouragement." What could you say to encourage someone?

Pray 💬

The believers in Jerusalem praised God every day. Say a prayer of praise, adding motions to go with your prayer.

Practice Peace 🕊

The believers in Jerusalem made sure that everyone had what they needed. Many people in our world do not have enough food, clean water, or money. What can be done about this?

Daily Bread

ACTS 6:1-7

THE GROUP OF BELIEVERS in Jerusalem grew quickly. Different groups of people became part of one church. Some spoke Greek. Others spoke Aramaic. Some had been born in Jerusalem. Others had moved there from far away. These groups of people were different, yet they worshiped, prayed, and ate together. They shared everything.

Every day, the church gave out food. But over time a problem arose. The Greek-speaking widows were not receiving their share of food. Everyone in the church was supposed to be cared for, but that was not happening. What should be done? The people brought the problem to the 12 apostles.

The apostles called everyone together and said, "As leaders, we need to spend our time praying and teaching people about Jesus, not handing out food. But it is very important that everyone has enough to eat. So choose seven wise people who are full of the Spirit. Put them in charge of giving out the food."

This made everyone happy. The apostles laid hands on the chosen workers and prayed. Then the seven workers made sure that everyone got their share of food.

God's word kept on spreading. Many people in Jerusalem, including many priests, became believers.

Wonder & Share

▶ I wonder why one group of widows was not getting enough food.

▶ Give an example of something that is fair and an example of something that is unfair.

Pray

Choose a snack food that is easy to divide, such as crackers or grapes. Give a snack item to another person as you pray, being sure that everyone gets an equal amount. Take turns praying and sharing.

Peace Path
Love Your Neighbor

Look at the "Peace with Others" ideas on pages 352–353. Which ones were used in this Bible story? What else might have helped them solve their problem?

This is the end of the path! Go to **PAGE 16** to choose another peace path.

The Road to Ethiopia

ACTS 8:5-6, 26-40

THE CHURCH BEGAN to face challenges. Not everyone had the same beliefs, and there were even people who wanted to hurt the believers. Still the believers went from place to place, telling everyone about Jesus. Philip traveled to the city of Samaria, where he preached and healed many people. The crowds listened eagerly.

Then an angel of God said to Philip, "Go to the wilderness road that leads from Jerusalem to Gaza." Philip went.

An important official was traveling on that road in his chariot. He had been worshiping in Jerusalem but was now going home to Ethiopia, where he had important work to do. He was in charge of all the money and jewels in Queen Candace's treasury.

On the way, the Ethiopian official was reading from the scroll of the prophet Isaiah. Philip ran up to the chariot and heard him reading from the scroll. "Do you understand what you are reading?" Philip asked him.

The official replied, "How can I? I need someone to guide me. Come sit in my chariot and listen to these words from the prophet Isaiah:

'Like a sheep, he was led to his death.
Like a lamb, he was quiet and did not open his mouth.
He did not receive justice. His life was taken away.'

"Who was Isaiah talking about? Himself or someone else?" asked the official.

Philip said, "Isaiah was talking about Jesus, the Son of God. Even though Jesus had done nothing wrong, he was killed. But then, by the power of God, he was raised to life again!"

They came to some water and the official said, "Stop here! I want to be baptized." The two men went into the water and Philip baptized him. Then the Spirit of God suddenly took Philip away. The official went on his way with great joy.

Wonder & Share

▶ Imagine going from place to place telling people about Jesus.

▶ Whom could you talk to if you had questions about the Bible?

Pray 💬

Pray for someone who is different from you—someone from a different school or city, someone with a different skin color, or even someone who disagrees with you.

Peace Path
God Welcomes All

The angel of God sent Philip to make sure that the official from a foreign country understood what he was reading in the book of Isaiah. God's message was not just for people who lived in Israel. It was for everyone.

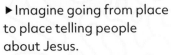 **PAGE 306**

Saul and the Heavenly Light

ACTS 8:1B–3; 9:1–31

THE CHURCH IN JERUSALEM grew quickly—so quickly that some people wanted to stop it. A young man named Saul went from house to house, dragging followers of Jesus off to prison. At Saul's request, the high priest gave him permission to bring all believers back to Jerusalem in chains. Saul set out for Damascus.

As Saul came close to the city, a light from heaven flashed around him. He fell to the ground. A voice said, "Saul, Saul, why do you persecute me?"

Saul said, "Who is speaking to me?"

The voice said, "I am Jesus, the one you are persecuting. Get up and go into the city, and you will be told what to do next." Saul got up but could see nothing. He had been blinded. Saul's friends led him into the city. For three days Saul did not eat or drink.

There was a believer in Damascus named Ananias. God called him in a vision, saying, "Go to Judas' house on Straight Street. Saul is praying there."

Ananias was afraid. "Saul has done terrible things to the believers in Jerusalem!" he said.

God said, "Go. I have chosen Saul. He will speak to Jews, Gentiles, and even kings about me."

So Ananias went and found Saul. He laid his hands on Saul and prayed for him. Immediately Saul could see again, and he was baptized as a follower of Jesus.

Saul taught about Jesus in the synagogue, and many people were amazed to see that he had changed. Later, other people planned to kill Saul. But his disciples lowered Saul in a large basket through an opening in the city wall, and he escaped to Jerusalem.

The disciples in Jerusalem were afraid of Saul. Did he really believe in Jesus, or would he hurt them? After Barnabas told them what happened to Saul on the road, they trusted him, and he began teaching in their synagogues.

The churches in Judea, Galilee, and Samaria were at peace and grew through the power of the Holy Spirit.

Wonder & Share

▶ I wonder why Saul wanted to put people in prison because of what they believed.
▶ Ananias prayed for Saul. Share about a time you prayed for someone.

Pray

First Saul hated followers of Jesus. Then he changed and became a follower! Use the finger path on page 347 as you pray. As you move to the middle, think of something wrong you have done. As you move back out, think of God's love and forgiveness.

Dig In

Saul's name was later changed to Paul. He traveled to many cities, such as Salamis, Paphos, Perga, Antioch, Iconium, Lystra, and Derbe to tell people about Jesus. Find the cities on the map on pages 370–371.

Tabitha

ACTS 9:36-43

TABITHA WALKED ALONG THE SHORE of the Mediterranean Sea, watching as the boats arrived in the port of her hometown of Joppa. The sight of children splashing in the water brought a smile to her face.

Back at home, Tabitha began sewing. She was making a robe for her neighbor, whose husband had recently died. It was hard to have young children and no husband.

By the middle of the day, Tabitha was not feeling well. She had to set her sewing aside and rest. But rest did not help. She felt worse. Her family brought food, but she could not eat it. Days passed. Finally, they sent for the doctor, but nothing more could be done.

Tabitha's family and friends gathered around, weeping, praying, and hoping for a miracle. But their beloved Tabitha died. They washed her body and laid it in an upstairs room.

The disciples heard that Peter was near Joppa. They sent two men to ask him to come quickly. Peter came to Tabitha's home. Her friends wept, showing him the robes and other clothing Tabitha had made for them. They told him what a kind and generous woman she was—always caring for others.

Peter went to the upstairs room and asked everyone to leave. He knelt and prayed, then said "Tabitha, get up." She opened her eyes, saw Peter, and sat up. He took her by the hand and helped her up. Peter called all the friends, disciples, and widows to see that Tabitha was alive!

Many people in Joppa believed in Jesus because of what happened to Tabitha.

Wonder & Share

▶ I wonder what other kind and generous things Tabitha did.

▶ How do people care for you when you are sick?

Pray

Choose one of the "Ways to Pray" from pages 340–341. Do that as you pray for people who are sick.

Dig In 📖

Joppa was an important city in the Old Testament. Cedar trees used to build Solomon's temple came through the port in Joppa. (Read about the building of the temple on pages 90–93.) Jonah also went to Joppa to board a ship for Tarshish. (Read his story on page 144.)

Good News for All

ACTS 10

CORNELIUS LIVED IN CAESAREA. He was an officer in the Roman army. Cornelius and his household had learned to know God. He prayed often and gave freely to everyone who was in need.

One day, Cornelius saw a vision of an angel. The angel told Cornelius to send for Peter, who was in Joppa. Cornelius sent two of his enslaved men and a soldier to Joppa.

The next day in Joppa, Peter went to pray on the rooftop. He felt hungry. Then Peter had a vision. He saw something like a large sheet lowered from heaven to the ground. Animals, birds, and reptiles were inside.

"Peter," a voice said. "You may kill and use these animals for food."

"No, Lord," Peter protested. "These animals are not good to eat." The Jewish people—who followed the important instructions God gave Moses—did not eat the animals Peter saw.

But the voice insisted. "God has called them good. You must not call them anything else."

Peter felt confused. Suddenly, Cornelius' men arrived.

"Go meet those men," the Spirit of God told Peter.

Peter listened and traveled to Cornelius' house with the men. When Peter arrived, many of Cornelius' friends and family were there. Peter said to them, "Normally Jews and Gentiles do not visit or eat with one another. But God showed me that all people are good, despite our differences. I am learning that God does not favor one group of people over another. Everyone who follows God and does what is right is welcome in God's family, no matter where they come from. God sent Jesus to be a peacemaker and to forgive us our wrongs—Jesus is for everyone."

The Holy Spirit swept through the place. All the people—both Jews and Gentiles—began to speak in other languages and praise God. What a surprise! Even though they weren't Jews like Peter, he baptized them in the name of Jesus. The Spirit's visit was a great gift for everyone.

Wonder & Share 💡

▶ I wonder why Jews and Gentiles often avoided each other.

▶ Share about a friendship you have with someone who is different from you.

Pray 💬

Imagine two groups of people who don't like each other. They are far apart. Use blocks or other materials to build a bridge as you pray for peace between the two groups. Imagine them meeting in peace on your bridge.

Peace Path 🔥

God Welcomes All

Peter, who was Jewish, learned that God does not have favorites. God did not love him more than Cornelius, who was a Gentile. God loved both Peter and Cornelius.

🐍 This is the end of the path! Go to **PAGE 16** to choose another peace path.

Lydia

ACTS 16:11–15, 40

EARLY EACH MORNING, Lydia went to the shores of the Mediterranean Sea in search of shellfish. She needed them to make purple dye for the cloth she sold. Wealthy people came from far and wide to buy her beautiful purple cloth.

On the Sabbath, Lydia, her family, and her friends went outside the gate of the city to the river. They met there to pray every week. Two men came up and asked to sit with them. It was Paul and Silas, who had recently arrived in Philippi. Paul said, "God gave me a vision, telling us to come and share the good news here."

"What is this good news?" Lydia asked.

The two men told them about Jesus, the teacher and healer who was the Son of God. Lydia listened eagerly, amazed to learn that God had raised Jesus to life after three days in the tomb. The men explained how the followers of Jesus were baptized with water and the Holy Spirit.

God opened Lydia's heart. She wanted to be baptized too, along with her family. So Paul and Silas baptized them in the river. Filled with joy, Lydia said, "Please come and stay in my home." So they did.

Paul and Silas traveled to other places in the region of Macedonia for some time. Before leaving, they returned to Lydia's house. They encouraged the believers from the church and then went on their way.

Wonder & Share

▶ I wonder why Lydia and her family went to the river to pray. Where is a special place your family could pray?

▶ Tell about a time you were excited to learn something new, like Lydia was.

Pray

Fill a glass with water. Add red and blue food coloring to make the water purple like the dye Lydia made. Slowly pour out the purple water as you pray for people who have not yet heard the good news about Jesus.

Dig In

Philippi was originally named *Crenides*, which means "fountains" in Greek. When King Philip II of Macedon conquered the city in 356 BC, he renamed it Philippi. There was a theater there, as well as gold mines nearby.

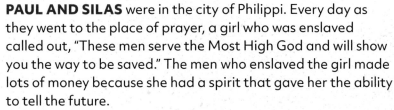

Paul and Silas

ACTS 16:16-39

PAUL AND SILAS were in the city of Philippi. Every day as they went to the place of prayer, a girl who was enslaved called out, "These men serve the Most High God and will show you the way to be saved." The men who enslaved the girl made lots of money because she had a spirit that gave her the ability to tell the future.

After many days, Paul said to the spirit inside the girl, "In the name of Jesus, come out of her." And it happened. The girl was free from having to tell the future. The men who enslaved her were furious. They could no longer make any money from her. So they dragged Paul and Silas to the Roman leaders, who had them beaten and thrown in prison.

At midnight, Paul and Silas were praying and singing hymns as the other prisoners listened. Suddenly a violent earthquake shook the prison. The doors opened, and everyone's chains came unfastened.

The jailer woke up and saw that the prison doors were open. He thought all the prisoners had escaped, and he would be punished for not doing his job. Afraid, he grabbed his sword, ready to kill himself. But Paul shouted to him, "Do not hurt yourself! We are all here."

The jailer dropped to his knees before Paul and Silas. "What must I do to be saved?" he asked.

"Believe in Jesus, and you and your whole household will be saved," they replied.

The jailer brought Paul and Silas to his home. He washed their wounds and fed them. Paul and Silas taught the man and his family about Jesus. They were all baptized and rejoiced.

The next morning, Paul and Silas had returned to prison, and the Roman leaders sent police to free them. But Paul refused to leave, saying, "The Roman leaders beat us and threw us in prison without a trial! The leaders must come and free us themselves." So the leaders came and apologized to Paul and Silas, then set them free.

The two men went back to Lydia's house, where they met with other followers of Jesus.

Wonder & Share

▶ I wonder why Paul and Silas were up at midnight praying and singing.
▶ The leaders apologized to Paul and Silas for wrongly putting them in prison. Tell about a time you said, "I'm sorry."

Pray

Paul later wrote a letter to the church in Philippi. (See page 322.) He wrote, "Instead of worrying, pray and ask God for what you need. Give thanks for what you have." Follow Paul's instructions: Ask God for what you need and give thanks.

Live It

Paul and Silas sang together during a hard situation. Make a list of songs that will comfort you when you are upset or having a hard day.

Preaching in Corinth

AFTER LEAVING PHILIPPI, Paul and Silas went to Thessalonica and Beroea. Silas stayed in Beroea while Paul continued to Athens and then to Corinth.

In Corinth, Paul met Aquila and Priscilla, a couple who had recently moved to Corinth from Italy. They were tentmakers, and Paul stayed and worked with them.

Every Sabbath, Paul met with people in the synagogue, trying to convince them that Jesus was the Messiah, the one sent from God to save them. Paul's preaching made many Jewish people very angry, and they turned against him.

Paul said, "From now on, I will preach to the Gentiles. They are not Jewish like me, but I want them to hear the good news of Jesus."

Paul went to the home of Titius Justus, a Gentile who worshiped God and lived next door to the synagogue. Crispus, a synagogue leader, and his whole family believed in Jesus. Many other Corinthians also became followers of Jesus and were baptized after hearing Paul preach.

One night, God came to Paul in a vision and said, "Do not be afraid. Keep on speaking and do not be silent. I am with you and will protect you. No one will harm you, for many people here believe in me."

Paul stayed in Corinth for 18 months, teaching the word of God.

After leaving Corinth, Paul wrote letters to the Corinthian church to encourage and teach them. In one letter, he wrote:

"Beloved family, God has been close to the churches of Philippi, Thessalonica, and Beroea. They had hard, painful times, yet still were joyful. They became poor but still gave generously. You too are filled with faith, wisdom, and love. Now excel in giving, just as Jesus did!

Right now, you have plenty, so share with others. Later, others can share with you if you have needs. This creates a fair balance so that everyone is cared for.

Remember this: If you plant a little, you will gather a little. If you plant a lot, you will gather a lot. Give freely, not because you are forced to give but because you want to give. God loves it when we give joyfully. God will provide for you so that you can share generously."

Wonder & Share

▶ I wonder why some people did not want Paul in their synagogue.

▶ It's not always easy to share. What can make it hard to give to others?

Pray

Aquila, Priscilla, and Paul were tentmakers. Use blankets, sheets, or other things around your house to make a tent. Go inside to pray.

Dig In

Paul preached in Philippi, Thessalonica, Beroea, Athens, and Corinth. Find these cities on the map on pages 370–371.

One Body, Many Gifts

ROMANS 12:1-8

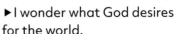

PAUL WROTE A LETTER to the church in Rome:

"To all God's beloved children in Rome: Grace and peace to you from Jesus Christ.

Worship and serve God with your whole being: heart, soul, body, and mind. Don't become like the world around you. Let God transform you! Then you will understand things in a completely new way. You will discover all that God desires for the world.

I say to every one of you, think carefully about the kind of person you are. God has given you the gift of faith. Let that faith guide you. A body has many parts. Each part has an important job to do. That's how it is in the church, which is the body of Jesus Christ. There are many people, but we are all part of Christ's body and part of each other. God has given each person gifts to use. So use your gifts! If you have the gift of helping others, then help. If you can teach, then teach. If you can comfort people, then comfort them. If you can give, then give as much as you can. If you are a leader, then do your very best. If you can take care of others, then do it happily."

Wonder & Share ☀

▶ I wonder what God desires for the world.
▶ What jobs need to be done in a church? Which one interests you most?

Pray 💬

Ask God to show you what gifts you have. Then draw a picture of yourself using one of your gifts.

Peace Path
I Am Special

God has given you special gifts! Can you help, teach, comfort, give, lead, or take care of people? Can you build, share, create, cook, paint, draw, make music, dance, write, design, count, observe, pray, imagine, or read?

This is the end of the path! Go to **PAGE 16** to choose another peace path.

Love Is . . .

1 CORINTHIANS 1:10–11; 13:1–13

PAUL WROTE A LETTER to the church in Corinth:

"Beloved children, I have heard news that there are many arguments in your church. I ask you to be in agreement in the name of our Lord Jesus Christ. I do not want anything to separate you. Be united in the same mind and goals together. What I want to tell you is this:

If I can speak in all the languages of people, and even angels, but do not have love, I am just a clanging cymbal. If I have the gifts of prophecy, knowledge, and amazing faith, but do not have love to unite it all, those gifts don't matter. What if I give away all the things I own and give my own body as a sacrifice so I can brag about how great I am? If I do not have love, it means nothing.

Love is patient. Love is kind. Love is not jealous, boastful, prideful, or rude. Love does not demand its own way. It is not easily irritated and does not hold grudges. Love does not rejoice in what is wrong but rejoices in the truth. Love can stand anything. It believes in every true thing and hopes in everyone. Love is true everywhere. Love never ends.

Prophecies, speaking in other languages, and great knowledge will all come to an end. But love is forever. Right now, we only know a part of what is happening, but when The Complete One comes, all will be made whole.

When I was a child, I spoke like a child, I thought like a child, and then I became an adult. For now, things are unclear, like looking into a foggy mirror. But one day we will have true and clear understanding. Even I, Paul, only know a part of what is happening. Someday I will know things fully, and I will be fully known by God.

Faith, hope, and love stay with us, and the greatest of these is love."

Wonder & Share

▶ I wonder what new things we will learn about God as we keep growing.
▶ Share about a time you were patient, kind, trusting, or hopeful.

Pray 💬

Breathe on a mirror to make it foggy. Tell God about a time you failed to show love. Now wipe the mirror clean so you can see your face clearly. Say, "God forgives me and loves me."

Live It ☀

We don't know everything about God, but we do know some things. Finish this sentence: **God, you are**_____.

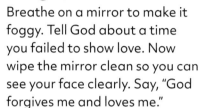

Jesus Is Our Peace

EPHESIANS 2:12-22

PAUL WROTE A LETTER to the church in Ephesus:

"Grace and peace to you from Christ Jesus!

Remember when you didn't know about Christ Jesus? You were not born into a Jewish family. You did not know about God's holy promises. In a world without God's promises, you could not have hope. But now, because of Jesus, you can belong to God's family.

Jesus brought us together in peace. We are different from each other, but now we are one people. Jesus broke down the wall of hate between us when he died on the cross. He brought peace between us and God. Jesus' words of peace are for everyone! Even people who believe different things. Even people who don't sound or look like family. Everyone can share peace because of Jesus.

And all people can come to God because of Jesus and God's Spirit. Now you aren't strangers anymore—you are members of God's family. We are like a house. God used the prophets and apostles to build the foundation. Jesus is the most important stone, the one that holds the whole house together. You are being made into a house where God lives through the Spirit!"

Wonder & Share

▶ I wonder how Jesus shares peace with us. How can we share peace with others?
▶ I wonder if you've ever felt different from the people around you. What makes you feel welcome and part of a group?

Pray

Build a wall with blocks. As you pray for peace in your family, community, and the world, remove the blocks one at a time.

Peace Path
Love Your Enemies

Sometimes when we disagree, argue, or have been hurt by someone, it can feel like there is a wall between us and that person. What can be done to break down that sort of wall?

This is the end of the path! Go to **PAGE 16** to choose another peace path.

God Is Near

PHILIPPIANS 4:1–14

PAUL WROTE A LETTER to the church in Philippi:

"Grace and peace to you from Jesus Christ!

Beloved family, I love and miss you. You are my joy and crown. Be strong in the Lord!

I heard that Euodia and Syntyche have been arguing. I urge them to come together so they can work out their disagreement and understand one another. Help these women. They worked hard with me, sharing the good news of Jesus with many people. Take care of them, along with Clement and the other workers.

Be filled with joy, friends. I will say it again: Be filled with joy!

Let everyone see that you are kind and gentle. God is near to you. Instead of worrying, pray and ask God for what you need. Give thanks for what you have. Then God's peace will fill your heart and your mind.

Beloved, think about things that are good and true, right and fair, beautiful and worthy of praise.

Keep on doing the things that I have taught you. The God of peace will always be with you.

Thank you for sharing in my hard times. I have learned how to be happy with what I have. I have been hungry, and I have had plenty of food. I have been poor and had more than enough. I am at peace no matter what happens. I can go through anything because Jesus gives me strength."

Wonder & Share ☀

▶ I wonder what the two women disagreed about. What might have helped them understand each other better?

▶ Name something that is true, something that is fair, and something that is worthy of praise.

Pray 💬

Give thanks for what you have. Then imagine God's peace filling your heart and mind.

Peace Path

I Need Comfort

Next time you feel worried or are having a hard time, remember that God is near to you. Jesus can give you strength for any struggle, big or small.

〰 This is the end of the path! Go to **PAGE 16** to choose another peace path.

New Clothes and A New Song

COLOSSIANS 3:10–17

PAUL WROTE A LETTER to the church in Colossae:

"You are becoming new as you learn more about God and God's ways. It's like putting on fresh, new clothes—God's clothes! In God's way, no matter what country you are from, what family you belong to, whether you are enslaved or free, or anything else about you—Christ Jesus is for everyone.

As God's holy and beloved people, put on God's clothes of compassion, kindness, humility, gentleness, and patience. Be understanding of each other. If one of you hurts the other, forgive. The Lord has forgiven you, so you must also forgive.

Above everything else, put on clothes of love. Love ties everything together, like a perfect song. Let the peace of Christ be your heart's rule. And be thankful.

Let Christ's words live with you. Teach Christ's words and remind each other of them with wisdom. With thankfulness in your hearts, sing songs, hymns, and spiritual songs to God.

And whatever you do or say, let it be in thankfulness to God through the name of the Lord Jesus."

Wonder & Share

▶ Imagine putting on love like you put on a shirt!
▶ What three things are you thankful for today?

Pray

Say a forgiveness prayer. Ask God to help you forgive someone else or ask for God's forgiveness. Thank God for forgiving you.

Live It

Sing songs together with a grateful heart for all that God has done!

All Are Welcome

JAMES 1:27–2:8, 14–17

JAMES WROTE A LETTER to Jewish followers of Jesus living in Gentile lands:

"If you want to be a true follower of God, then do this: Care for orphans and widows when they are experiencing hard times. And stay away from things that distract you from God's way of love.

Beloved family, is it right to think that one person is better than another? Is that the way of Jesus? Imagine that a person with gold rings and fancy clothes comes into your gathering. And then a person wearing dirty clothes who has no money comes. Will you give special treatment and a seat of honor to the person in fancy clothes, while telling the other person to 'Stand over there' or 'Sit on the floor by my feet?' If you do this, you are picking favorites and judging people unfairly.

Listen, beloved family. God chooses people who are poor to have lasting faith and a place in God's kingdom. Yet you care more about people who have lots of money, even when they reject the name of God and make life hard for you.

Choose what is best: love your neighbor as yourself.

What good is it if you say, 'I have faith in God' and yet you don't take care of the people around you? What if someone has no clothes or food? Is it right to say, 'Go in peace! Stay warm and eat lots of food,' and yet give them nothing? What good are words without actions? Faith without acts of loving-kindness is dead."

Wonder & Share 💡
▶ I wonder what acts of loving-kindness you could do today.
▶ What could you say or do if you saw some children being treated better than others?

Pray 💬
Pray for people who have been treated unfairly or left out. If this has happened to you, read the messages on page 351 aloud to yourself as part of your prayer.

Practice Peace 🕊
Think about people in your school, church, or neighborhood. How can you help everyone feel welcome and included?

Love One Another

1 JOHN 4:7-21

BELOVED, LET US LOVE ONE ANOTHER, because love is from God. Everyone who loves is God's child and knows God. If we do not love we cannot know God, for God is love. How did God show love to us? God sent Jesus, the unique son, to this world so that we might find life. This is holy love. We did not love God, but God loved us and sent Jesus to forgive our wrongs. Beloved, since God loved us so much, we must love one another. No one has ever seen God. If we love one another, God helps make our love complete.

We know that we are with God and God is with us through the gift of the Holy Spirit. Think of everything we have seen and witnessed! God has sent the Son as the Savior of the world. God lives in those who believe that Jesus is the Son of God. Always remember and believe in the love God has for us.

God is love. When we stay in God's love, God stays in us. Love gives us boldness and takes away our fears. We love because God first loved us. If someone says, "I love God," but hates their family, they are not telling the truth. How can they be? If they cannot love their own family, whom they know in person, how can they love God, whom they have not seen? This is the commandment we have from God: people who love God must also love all others.

Wonder & Share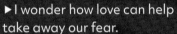

▶ I wonder how love can help take away our fear.

▶ Share a special memory about a person you love.

Pray 💬

Cut out paper hearts. Write the name of a person you want to pray for on each heart. Hang up the hearts as you pray for each person.

Dig In 📖

There are three letters from John in the Bible. The longest is 1 John, with five chapters. There are only 13 verses in 2 John, and 3 John only has 15 verses!

Worthy Is the Lamb

REVELATION 1:4–5A; 5:11–13; 7:9–17

MANY YEARS after Jesus' death and resurrection, followers of Jesus were being punished. They lived differently than their neighbors, and they did not worship the emperor of Rome. One man, John, was sent far away from his family and friends to the island of Patmos. John wrote a letter to the seven churches in Asia:

"Grace and peace to you from Jesus, the first one to overcome death and rule over all earthly kings.

God gave me a vision of thousands upon thousands of angels around the throne. Every creature in heaven, on earth, under the earth, and in the ocean sang loudly,

> 'Worthy is Jesus the Lamb to receive
>   power, wealth, wisdom, and might,
> honor, glory, and blessing
>   forever and ever!'

Then I saw a crowd of people—more than anyone could count. They were from every race, tribe, nation, and language. Dressed in white robes, they gathered before the throne and Jesus the Lamb. They waved palm branches and cried out, 'God and the Lamb have power to save all people.' The angels and elders fell on their faces before the throne and worshiped God.

The people in the crowd had gone through great suffering, but they still worshiped God both day and night. One of the elders said to me,

> 'The Lamb on the throne will spread a tent over them.
>   The sun and heat will not hurt them.
>   They will not be hungry or thirsty anymore.
> The Lamb will be their shepherd,
>   leading them to streams of living water.
> God will wipe all tears from their eyes.'"

Wonder & Share ☀

▶ Imagine all people and all creatures together in one place praising God.
▶ Which part of John's vision do you like best?

Pray 💬

Joyfully read the paragraph in the story that begins, "Worthy is Jesus the Lamb" as your prayer. Repeat it several times, starting with a whisper and getting louder each time.

Peace Path 🕊

I Am Not Alone

Reread the last paragraph that begins, "The Lamb on the throne." How will the people be cared for? Imagine God caring for you in those ways.

👉 This is the end of the path! Go to **PAGE 16** to choose another peace path.

A New Creation

REVELATION 21:1-7; 22:1-5, 16-17

WHILE JOHN WAS ON THE ISLAND OF PATMOS, he had another vision:

"I, John, saw a new heaven and a new earth. The holy city, a new Jerusalem, came down out of heaven from God. I heard a voice from the throne say,

> 'Look! God is now making a home with people.
>   God will wipe every tear from their eyes.
> No one will cry or be in pain or die anymore,
>   for the old way is gone now.
> Look! I am making everything new.
>   I am the Alpha and Omega,
>   the first and the last,
>   the beginning and the end.
> I will give living water to everyone who is thirsty.
>   I will be their God, and they will be my children.'

Then an angel showed me the river of living water, bright as crystal. It flows from the throne, down the street of the holy city. On either side of the river, there is a tree of life with 12 kinds of fruit. Its leaves will heal the nations. The throne of God and the Lamb is there. People joyfully worship as they look at the very face of God. There is no more night, and no need for a lamp. For God's light shines on everyone."

"It is I, Jesus, who sent my angel to you with this message for the churches. I am the descendant of King David and the bright morning star.

> The Spirit says 'Come.'
>   Let all who are thirsty come.
>   Let everyone receive the living water as a gift.
> Surely, I am coming soon."

Amen. Come, Lord Jesus!

Wonder & Share

▶ I wonder what God's face looks like.
▶ What would you change if you could make a new earth?

Pray

Draw a picture of John's vision as you pray.

Peace Path

Nature Trail

What things from nature are in John's vision? What is special about them? Look back at the first story in this story Bible. How is the new creation in John's vision like the first creation?

This is the end of the path! Go to **PAGE 16** to choose another peace path.

Thousands of years have
passed since John's vision.

All people and nations
do not yet live in peace.

But we can all work together
to make a more peaceful,
just, and beautiful world.

How will **you** be part of
God's never-ending story?

EXTRAS

Types of Prayer

thank you.

(gratitude)
Tell God what you are grateful for in your life.

I LOVE you.

(love)
Express your love for God.

help OTHERS.

(intercession)
Pray for people who are struggling, sad, sick, or in need of help.

HELP ME.

(petition)
Ask God for help with hard things happening in your life.

I AM sorry.

(confession)
We all do and say things that are wrong. Sometimes we also fail to do good things that we could do. Tell God about the wrong things you do. God will forgive you!

PRAISE YOU.

(praise)
Give praise for the amazing and special things God does.

something TERRIBLE happened. HELP ME understand.

(lament)
Difficult things happen in the world. Express your deep feelings and hard questions to God.

Ways to Pray

Movement prayer
Use your body to show your prayer. Dance, stretch, wave streamers, kneel, raise your arms, or make up motions that go along with your prayer.

Art prayer
Draw, paint, or doodle as you pray.

Alphabet prayer
Pray for someone or something that begins with each letter of the alphabet.

Clay or play dough prayer
Form the dough to show your prayer.

Color prayer
Thank God for something that is each color of the rainbow.

Writing prayer
Write the words of your prayer.

Nature prayer
Get out in nature as you pray or bring nature items inside to use while you pray.

"On the way" prayer
Pray while you are in the car, bus, train, subway, or airplane. Pray on a bike, in your wheelchair, or while you walk or run.

Listening prayer
Be silent and listen for God.

Sand prayer

Pour sand onto a plate or into a shallow container. Draw pictures or write words to show your prayers. Gently shake the plate or container to start a new prayer.

Musical prayer

Make up your own prayer song to the tune of a simple song like "Mary Had a Little Lamb." Listen to music as you pray. Sing a prayer song.

Finger prayer paths

Turn to pages 346–347 and use your finger to trace one of the prayer paths as you pray silently.

Map prayer

Look at a map and pray for places and people in your community and around the world.

Scripture prayer

Pray using the words of other people in the Bible, such as Hannah (page 74); David (pages 87, 89); Jonah (page 144); the psalmists (pages 148, 151, 152, 154, 155); Mary (page 164); and Jesus (page 234).

Building prayer

Take turns stacking blocks or LEGO® bricks. Each time you add a block, pray for a person or situation.

Breath prayer

See the examples on page 344.

Pray Through the Day

Morning Prayers

Good morning, loving God of all!
(*Stretch both arms overhead.*)
You listen every time I call.
(*Touch both ears.*)
You show the way for me to go.
(*Reach both arms down to the floor.*)
You fill me with your love to show.
(*Return to the original position and
stretch both arms out to the sides.*)

———————

On this day (*clap, clap, clap*)
we can say, (*stomp, stomp, stomp*)
"Have no fear. (*Clap, clap, clap.*)
God is near!" (*Stomp, stomp, stomp.*)
(*Repeat. Change the actions as desired.*)

———————

God, I woke up feeling _____.
I don't know what this day will bring.
Will I laugh, yell, cry, or sing?
I'm glad that you know everything.

Evening Prayers

Goodnight, God. The day is done.
It was good and full of fun.
Thank you for the joy you bring,
Thank you, God, for everything.

———————

Goodnight, God. It was a hard day.
Nothing seemed to go my way.
Give me peaceful sleep this night.
Keep me in your loving sight.

———————

Goodnight, God. I'm filled with fear.
I am worried. Are you here?
Fill me with your peace and light,
so I can sleep all through the night.

———————

Thank you for the dark of night,
for the stars that shine so bright.
Thank you for the rising moon.
I know that sleep is coming soon.

———————

Glad, Sad, Sorry Prayer
Think back over your day.
Tell God something that made you **glad**,
a time when you felt **sad**,
and something you are **sorry** for.

Prayers for Any Time

Blessing for Leaving Home
(*Rest your hand gently on the person's head or shoulder.*)
May God fill you with love.
May God surprise you with joy.
May God bless you with peace.

———

School Prayer
Open my mind so I can learn. (*Touch your head.*)
Open my heart so I can love. (*Make a heart shape with your hands.*)
Strengthen my body so I can work. (*Show your muscles.*)
Inspire my soul so I can create. (*Place both hands on your heart.*)

———

Prayer for a Hard Day
God, I do not like this day. (*Squeeze your fists tightly.*)
It's awful and that's all I'll say.
_____ (*feeling*) is how I really feel. (*Open your fists, palms up.*)
I need you to be close to me. (*Place both hands over your heart.*)

———

Prayer for When I'm Sick
God, give my body peace and rest.
I'm feeling sick and not my best.
You are right here next to me.
You will never, ever leave.

———

Nature Prayers (*Go outside for these prayers.*)

For clouds and blue skies, (*reach both hands overhead*)
for birds and butterflies, (*flap your arms like wings*)
for flowers and trees growing tall, (*crouch down, then slowly rise up*)
we thank you, God, for all! (*Extend your arms out to the sides.*)

Great Creator, you made a beautiful world.
I sense you all around me.
(*Pause to listen, look, touch, and smell.*)
Help me to care for your creation.

Meal Prayers

Thank you, God, for food to eat,
    for family and the friends we meet.
Bless this meal and bless our home.
Help us in your way to grow.

———

Thank you for the sun and rain.
Thank you for the crops of grain.
Thank you for the fruit on trees,
    for vegetables, for greens and seeds.

———

When I am hungry,
    may I know you are with me.
When I am full, let me give thanks.
When our food is almost gone,
    may there be enough.
When our table is full, help us share.

———

God of Life, we thank you
    for the food that fills us,
    for the home that shelters us,
    for the family that loves us.

———

For this food we soon will eat,
    for the people gathered here,
we give thanks and know that you
    will strengthen us for all we do.

———

From field, farm, or garden,
    from factory, market, or store,
    this food we eat is a gift from you.
We bless it and we call it good.

Breath Prayers

Breathe in slowly as you say or think
one of the names for God from the left
column. Breathe out slowly as you say or
think one of the phrases from the right
column. Repeat several times. Add your
own ideas to each column.

Breathe In	Breathe Out
Loving God	*give me peace*
God of light	*calm my heart*
Teacher	*fill me*
Creator	*lead me*
Shepherd	*help me*
God of peace	*comfort me*
Holy Spirit	*bring me joy*
Loving friend	*forgive me*
Healer	*give me strength*

The Lord's Prayer
Luke 11:2–4 (*CEV*)

Father, help us to honor your name.
Come and set up your kingdom.
Give us each day the food we need.
Forgive our sins, as we forgive everyone
    who has done wrong to us.
And keep us from being tempted.

The Lord's Prayer
Based on Matthew 6:9–13 (*ESV, NRSV*)

Our Father in heaven,
    hallowed be your name.
    Your kingdom come, your will be done
        on earth as it is in heaven.
    Give us this day our daily bread.
    And forgive us our sins,
        as we forgive those who sin
        against us.
    And lead us not into temptation,
        but deliver us from evil.
    For yours is the kingdom, the power,
        and the glory forever. Amen.

Finger Prayer Paths

Start at the top left or top right. Slowly move your finger along the path. Stop at each place and pray for the person or thing described next to it. Go in any order, praying for as many people or things as you want. Then return to your starting place.

Pray for your family.

STOP Pray for people around the world.

Pray for teachers.

Pray for people who are sick.

Pray for people at church.

Pray for your friends.

Pray for creation.

Start at the heart. Slowly follow the prayer path with your finger until you reach the middle. Pause in the middle. Then move backward until you reach the heart again. Speak your prayer aloud or think about it silently as you move your finger.

Peace with God

LOVE
Loving God with your heart, mind, soul, and strength is the most important thing.

PRAY
Share your joys, needs, hopes, doubts, praises, and concerns with God.

TRUST
Rely on God to be with you and keep the promises found in the Bible.

BELIEVE
Put your faith in Jesus, who shows us how to live and offers us eternal life.

LEARN
Read the Bible or talk to an adult about God. Notice how God is at work in the world.

WORSHIP
Connect with God through music and prayer.

FOLLOW

Live in a way that honors God. Choose God's right way of love.

ASK

Wonder about things. Be curious and ask God questions.

LISTEN

Be still and listen for God.

CONFESS

Tell God when you do things that are wrong.

REPENT

Turn away from what is wrong and do what is right.

Belong

Celebrate that you were lovingly created by God and belong in God's family.

PAUSE

Set aside time to be with God.

Peace Inside

Take long, slow breaths.

Draw your feelings.

Slowly count to 10.

Move (run, dance, stretch).

Squeeze play dough or a stress ball.

Pray.

Write your struggles in a journal.

Talk to a family member.

Smile or laugh.

Imagine God's peace filling you.

Be thankful.

Go to a peaceful place.

Listen to music.

Hug yourself.

Cry.

Read a book.

Talk to a friend.

Take care of your body.

Say kind words to yourself.

Build something.

Make art.

Play.

Hug someone.

Write a poem or song.

I am a CHILD of GOD.

I am SPECIAL to GOD.

I am MADE in GOD'S IMAGE.

I am LOVED NO matter WHAT.

Peace with Others

Try one of these ideas the next time you have a conflict or disagreement with a friend, family member, enemy, or even a stranger.

Surprise someone with kindness.

Refuse to fight.

Use "I" messages.

Respect everyone.

Go away and cool off.

Make new friends.

Speak up for what is right.

Ask for help.

Talk and listen.

Express your feelings and needs.

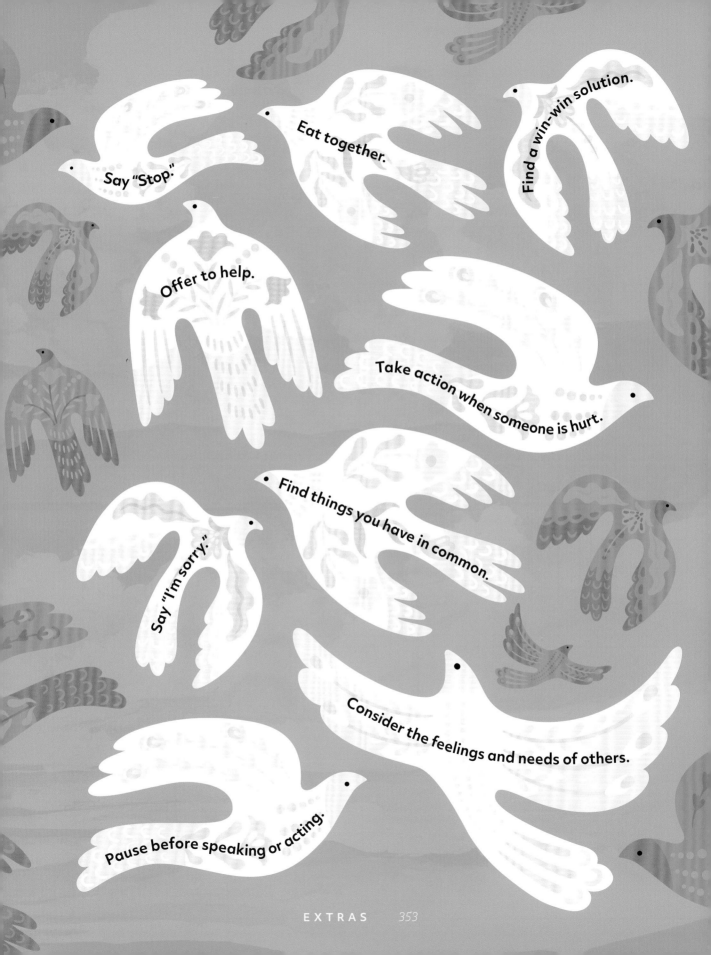

Peace with Creation

Take care of a plant.

Play outside and enjoy nature.

Celebrate the beauty of creation.

Thank God for creation.

Turn off the light when you leave a room.

Use less water.

Observe insects and animals.

Care for a pet.

Learn about creation through books and videos.

Pick up trash outside.

Walk or bike instead of using a car or bus.

Cut down on waste.

Weed a garden or flowerbed.

DONATE

Give away things you don't need anymore.

Plant a seed.

Reuse things instead of throwing them away.

Pray for endangered animals.

Books of the Bible

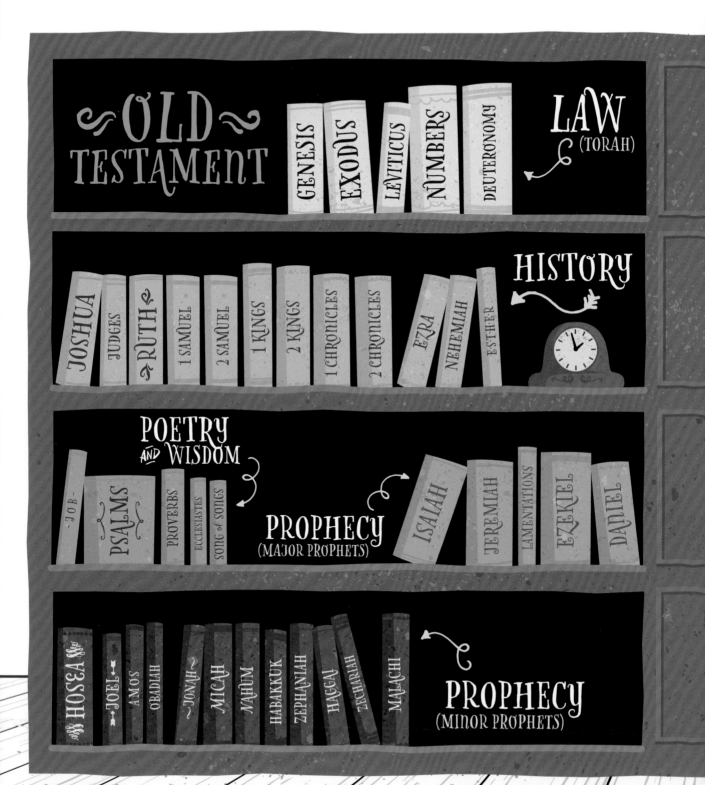

OLD TESTAMENT

GENESIS EXODUS LEVITICUS NUMBERS DEUTERONOMY

LAW (TORAH)

JOSHUA JUDGES RUTH 1 SAMUEL 2 SAMUEL 1 KINGS 2 KINGS 1 CHRONICLES 2 CHRONICLES EZRA NEHEMIAH ESTHER

HISTORY

POETRY AND WISDOM

JOB PSALMS PROVERBS ECCLESIASTES SONG of SONGS

PROPHECY (MAJOR PROPHETS)

ISAIAH JEREMIAH LAMENTATIONS EZEKIEL DANIEL

HOSEA JOEL AMOS OBADIAH JONAH MICAH NAHUM HABAKKUK ZEPHANIAH HAGGAI ZECHARIAH MALACHI

PROPHECY (MINOR PROPHETS)

NEW TESTAMENT

GOSPELS

MATTHEW
MARK
LUKE
J·O·H·N

HISTORY

ACTS

LETTERS

ROMANS
1 CORINTHIANS
2 CORINTHIANS
GALATIANS
EPHESIANS
PHILIPPIANS
COLOSSIANS
1 THESSALONIANS
2 THESSALONIANS

1 TIMOTHY
2 TIMOTHY
TITUS +
PHILEMON
HEBREWS
+ JAMES +
1 PETER
2 PETER
1 JOHN
« 2 JOHN »
3 JOHN
JUDE
REVELATION

Old Testament

TIMELINE

God creates the world.

A flood covers the earth.

God frees the Israelites from slavery. (*c. 1290 BCE*)

The Israelites wander in the wilderness for 40 years.

King Saul, King David, and King Solomon rule the united kingdom of Israel. (*1050–930 BCE*)

Solomon's temple is built. (*950 BCE*)

Prophets offer hope to the people of Judah.

God promises Abraham and Sarah a large family (known as the Israelites).

The Egyptian Pharaoh enslaves the Israelites.

The Israelites enter the land of Canaan.

Judges and prophets lead the Israelites.

The Assyrians conquer Israel. (*722 BCE*)

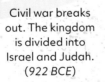

Civil war breaks out. The kingdom is divided into Israel and Judah. (*922 BCE*)

The Babylonians conquer Judah. The temple is destroyed. (*587 BCE*)

The people of Judah are exiled to Babylon.

King Cyrus allows the people of Judah to return to Israel. (*538 BCE*)

The people rebuild the temple. (*520–515 BCE*)

New Testament

TIMELINE

Jesus is born.
(*4 BCE*)

Jesus' family
flees to Egypt.

Jesus calls
disciples.

Jesus
teaches
and heals.

Jesus is
crucified.
(*c. 29 CE*)

Jesus is
raised
to life.

The church in
Jerusalem forms
and grows.

Paul starts
churches in
new places.

Jesus grows up in Israel.

Jesus is baptized.

Jesus enters Jerusalem on a donkey.

Jesus celebrates the Last Supper.

Jesus ascends to heaven.

The Holy Spirit comes at Pentecost.

The apostles write letters to the churches.

John has a vision of a new heaven and earth.

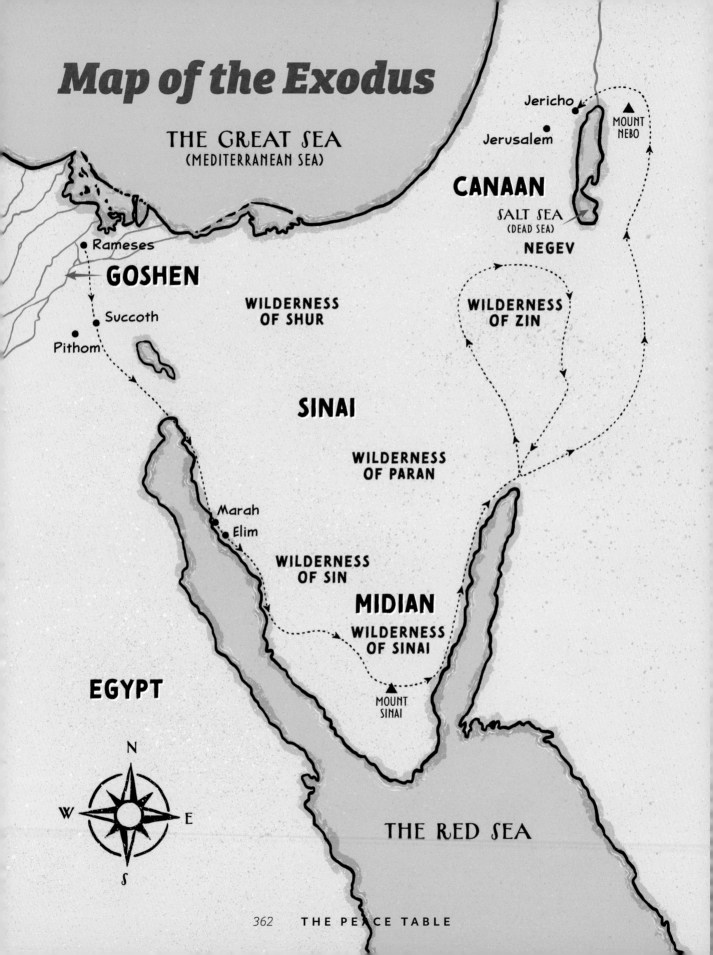

Map of the Exodus

THE GREAT SEA
(MEDITERRANEAN SEA)

CANAAN

Jericho

Jerusalem

MOUNT
NEBO

SALT SEA
(DEAD SEA)

NEGEV

Rameses

GOSHEN

WILDERNESS
OF SHUR

WILDERNESS
OF ZIN

Succoth

Pithom

SINAI

WILDERNESS
OF PARAN

Marah

Elim

WILDERNESS
OF SIN

MIDIAN

WILDERNESS
OF SINAI

EGYPT

MOUNT
SINAI

N

W   E

S

THE RED SEA

United Kingdom

ISRAEL

King Saul, King David, and King Solomon ruled over the united kingdom of Israel, 1050–930 BCE. Read about these kings on pages 78–85, 90–97.

ARAM

MEDITERRANEAN SEA

▲ MOUNT TABOR

KINGDOM OF ISRAEL

JORDAN RIVER

AMMON

Jericho ●

☆ Jerusalem

Bethlehem ●

▲ MOUNT NEBO

PHILISTIA

DEAD SEA

● Beersheba

MOAB

WILDERNESS OF ZIN

EDOM

N
W   E
S

Divided Kingdom

ISRAEL AND JUDAH

After Solomon's death, the country split into two kingdoms. The northern kingdom of Israel had 10 tribes. The southern kingdom of Judah had two tribes. For many years, the two kingdoms were at war with one another.

ARAM

MOUNT TABOR

KINGDOM OF ISRAEL

☆ SAMARIA

MEDITERRANEAN SEA

JORDAN RIVER

AMMON

Jericho

☆ JERUSALEM

Bethlehem

MOUNT NEBO

PHILISTIA

KINGDOM OF JUDAH

• Beersheba

DEAD SEA

MOAB

WILDERNESS OF ZIN

EDOM

N
W E
S

Northern Kingdom of Israel

- Named for Jacob (renamed Israel), the father of the 12 tribes (pages 34–39, 42–49)
- Ten tribes: Reuben, Simeon, Levi, Issachar, Zebulun, Gad, Asher, Dan, Naphtali, Joseph
- Capital: Samaria
- First king: Jeroboam
- Other famous king: Ahab (page 100)
- Conquered by the Assyrians in 722 BCE. The region then became known as Samaria.

Southern Kingdom of Judah

- Named for Judah, the fourth son of Jacob (page 42)
- Two tribes: Judah and Benjamin
- Capital: Jerusalem
- First king: Rehoboam (Solomon's son)
- Other famous kings: Josiah (page 104), Zedekiah (page 106)
- Conquered by the Babylonians in 587–586 BCE (page 106). The people of Judah were taken to Babylon as exiles. God sent many prophets to speak to them (pages 108–121). In 520 BCE, the people of Judah returned to rebuild Jerusalem (page 130–135).

Refer to the map on page 368 to see the land of Israel in the time of Jesus.

Solomon's Temple

(FIRST TEMPLE)

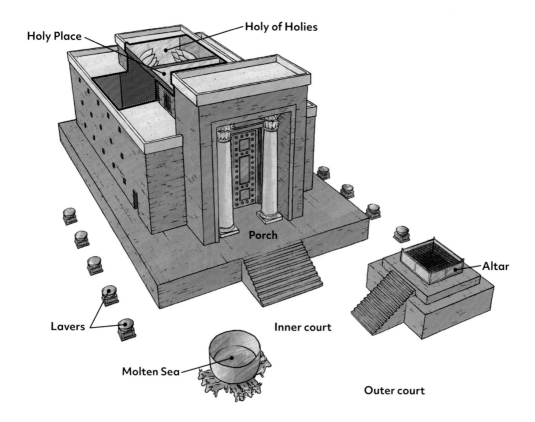

Holy Place — Holy of Holies — Porch — Altar — Lavers — Inner court — Molten Sea — Outer court

Solomon's temple was built around 950 BCE and was then destroyed in 587 BCE by the Babylonians.

The area outside the temple was divided into the Outer Court (Great Court) and Inner Court (Court of the Priests). People coming to worship at the temple gathered in the Outer Court. The Inner Court had a large altar, Molten Sea laver (water basin), and 10 other water basins. The Molten Sea laver was made of brass or bronze. Priests purified themselves by washing in it.

The temple was made up of the porch, the Holy Place, and the Holy of Holies. Storage rooms for the priests surrounded the temple.

The Holy Place had a gold-covered altar of incense, table of showbread, and seven-branched lampstand. The cedar walls had carvings of angels, trees, and flowers, which were covered with gold. The floor was overlaid with gold.

A colorful curtain separated the Holy Place from the Holy of Holies, where the Ark of the Covenant was kept. The tablets of the Ten Commandments were inside the ark. Large golden cherubim (angels) were placed above the ark. Only the high priest was allowed to go into the Holy of Holies once a year on Yom Kippur.

Herod's Temple

(SECOND TEMPLE)

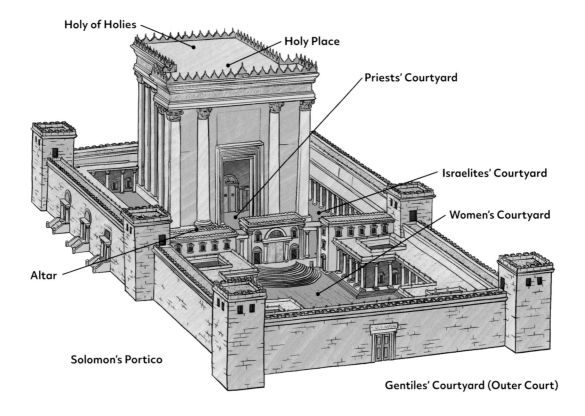

Holy of Holies

Holy Place

Priests' Courtyard

Israelites' Courtyard

Women's Courtyard

Altar

Solomon's Portico

Gentiles' Courtyard (Outer Court)

Originally the second temple was a small building built between 520–515 BCE by those who returned from exile in Babylon. It was renovated and expanded by King Herod the Great beginning in 20 BCE. It was more than twice the size of Solomon's temple. The temple was destroyed by the Romans in 70 CE.

Like in Solomon's temple, there was a large altar in front of the temple, and there was a porch, Holy Place, and Holy of Holies inside.

In the Holy Place, there was the golden lampstand, table of showbread, and golden altar of incense. Only priests could go into the Holy Place.

The Holy of Holies was empty because the Ark of the Covenant was no longer there. No one knows if it was hidden or stolen when the first temple was destroyed by the Babylonians. The high priest was allowed to go into the Holy of Holies once a year on Yom Kippur.

There were a variety of courtyards surrounding the temple. They indicated who was allowed to go in that area of the temple: Priests' Courtyard, Women's Courtyard, Israelites' Courtyard, and Gentiles' Courtyard.

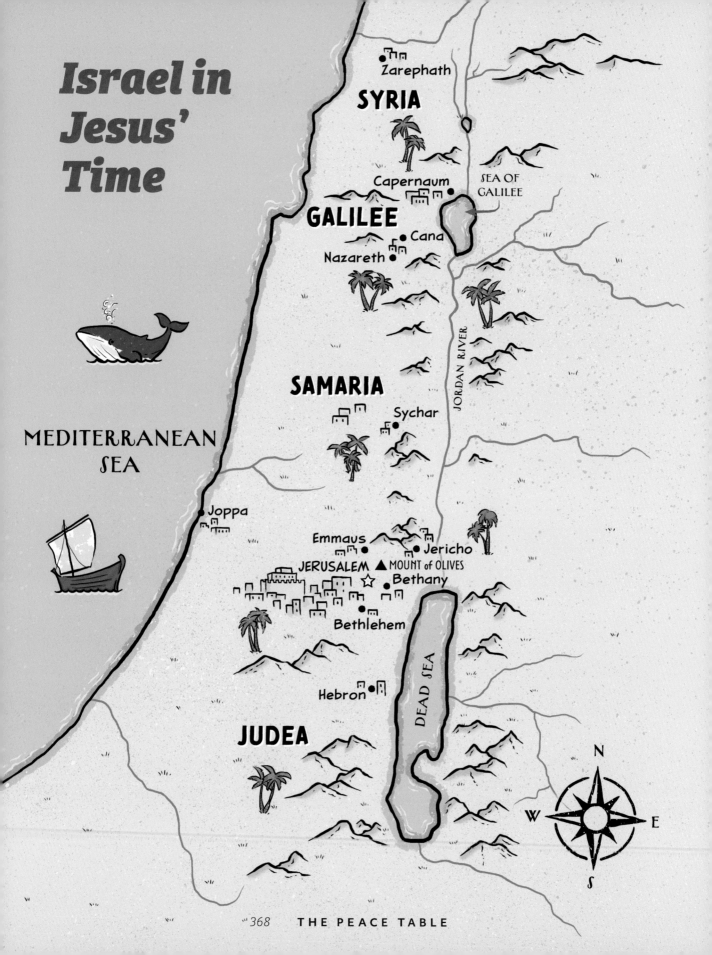

Israel in Jesus' Time

SYRIA

Zarephath

GALILEE

Capernaum

SEA OF GALILEE

Cana

Nazareth

MEDITERRANEAN SEA

SAMARIA

Sychar

JORDAN RIVER

Joppa

Emmaus

Jericho

JERUSALEM ▲ MOUNT of OLIVES

Bethany

Bethlehem

DEAD SEA

Hebron

JUDEA

N
W   E
S

The Events of Holy Week

The events leading up to Jesus' death and resurrection are often called Holy Week.

Sunday

Jesus entered Jerusalem, riding on a donkey. This is often called the Triumphal Entry and is celebrated on Palm Sunday.

Monday

Jesus went to the temple. It looked more like a market than a place of worship. Jesus overturned the tables. He taught that it was to be a house of worship for all people.

Tuesday

Wednesday

A woman anointed Jesus with perfume while he was having dinner at Simon's house.

Thursday

Jesus and his disciples shared the Last Supper. Later that evening Jesus was arrested in the Garden of Gethsemane. This is called Maundy Thursday.

Friday

Jesus was put on trial before the high priest, Herod, and Pilate. Even though he had done nothing wrong, he was condemned to die. Jesus was crucified, died, and was buried. This is called Good Friday.

Saturday

Jesus' friends and followers grieved his death. All hope seemed lost. Women prepared spices to put on Jesus' body.

Sunday

Jesus rose from the dead through the power of God. He appeared to his followers, including Mary Magdalene and other women. This is Easter!

MACEDONIA

ADRIATIC SEA

ITALY

☆ Rome

Philippi
Amphipolis ☆
Apollonia   Neapolis
Thessalonica
SAMOTHRACE
Beroea

GREECE

AEGEAN SEA

SICILY

Athens

Corinth ☆
Cenchreae

CRETE

The Church Grows

The apostle Paul traveled to more than 50 cities, talking to people about Jesus. This map shows two of his missionary journeys which both began at Antioch in Syria. Along the way, Paul started churches. He and other apostles later wrote letters to the churches to encourage them and help them know how to follow Jesus. *The Peace Table* includes letters to churches in Rome (page 316), Corinth (pages 315, 318–319), Ephesus (page 320), Philippi (page 322), and Colossae (page 324). These cities are marked with a star on the map.

Paul's first journey
– – – – – – – – – – –

Paul's second journey
– – – – – – – – – – –

BLACK SEA

GALATIA

Troas

Ephesus

PATMOS

Colossae

Antioch in Pisidia

Iconium

Lystra

Derbe

Tarsus

Attalia

Perga

Antioch

Seleucia Pieria

SYRIA

CYPRUS

Salamis

Paphos

MEDITERRANEAN SEA

Tyre

Caesarea Maritima

ISRAEL

Jerusalem

Pronunciation Guide

Abednego: *Uh-BED-ni-goh*

Abimelech: *uh-BIM-uh-lek*

Ahasuerus: *Uh-HAS-yoo-AIR-uhs*

Ananias: *AN-uh-NI-uhs*

Antioch: *AN-tee-ahk*

Aramaic: *Air-uh-MAY-ik*

Arimathea: *AIR-uh-muh-THEE-uh*

Babylon: *BAB-uh-lahn*

Barsabbas: *Bahr-SAB-uhs*

Bartimaeus: *Bahr-tuh-MEE-uhs*

Bartholomew: *Bahr-THOL-uh-myoo*

Beatitudes: *Bee-AT-uh-toodz*

Beersheba: *BEE-uhr-SHEE-buh*

Beroea: *Bi-REE-uh*

Caesarea: *SES-uh-REE-uh*

Canaan: *KAY-nuhn*

Capernaum: *Kuh-PUHR-nay-uhm*

Colossae: *Kuh-LOS-ee*

Cornelius: *Kor-NEEL-yuhs*

Derbe: *DUHR-bee*

Eleazar: *EL-ee-AY-zuhr*

Eliab: *I-LI-uhb*

Elimelech: *I-LIM-uh-lek*

Eliphaz: *EL-i-faz*

Elkanah: *el-KAY-nuh*

Euodia: *Yoo-OH-dee-uh*

Ezekiel: *I-ZEE-kee-uhl*

Gabriel: *GAY-bree-uhl*

Gerar: *GEE-rahr*

Golgotha: *GOL-guh-thuh*

Haman: *HAY-muhn*

Hilkiah: *Hil-KI-uh*

Hoglah: *HOG-luh*

Iconium: *I-KOH-nee-uhm*

Ishmael: *ISH-may-uhl*

Jairus: *JAY-i-ruhs*

Jericho: *JAIR-uh-koh*

Jeshua: *JESH-yoo-uh*

Jochebed: *JOK-uh-bed*

Josiah: *Joh-SI-uh*

Lazarus: *LAZ-uh-ruhs*

Lystra: *LIS-truh*

Macedonia: *MAS-uh-DOH-nee-uh*

Magi: *MAJ-ai*

Matthias: *Muh-THI-uhs*

Mediterranean:
 MED-i-tuh-RAY-nee-uhn

Mephibosheth: *mi-FIB-oh-sheth*

Meshach: *MEE-shak*

Messiah: *Muh-SI-uh*

Mica: *MI-kuh*

Mordecai: *MOR-duh-ki*

Nabal: *NAY-buhl*

Nebuchadnezzar:
 NEB-uh-kuhd-NEZ-uhr

Nehemiah: *NEE-hu-MI-uh*

Nicodemus: *NIK-uh-DEE-muhs*

Paphos: *PAY-fos*

Peninnah: *Pi-NIN-uh*

Pharaoh: *FAIR-oh*

Pharisees: *FAIR-uh-seez*

Philippi: *FIL-i-pi*

Potiphar: *POT-uh-fuhr*

Puah: *PYOO-uh*

Salamis: *SAL-uh-mis*

Samaria: *Suh-MAIR-ee-uh*

Sarai: *SAIR-i*

Shadrach: *SHAD-rak*

Shammah: *SHAM-uh*

Shaphan: *SHAY-fuhn*

Shechem: *SHEK-uhm*

Sheshbazzar: *Shesh-BAZ-uhr*

Shibah: *SHI-buh*

Shiphrah: *SHIF-ruh*

Shunem: *SHOO-nuhm*

Sinai: *SI-ni*

Sychar: *SI-kahr*

Syntyche: *SIN-ti-kee*

Thessalonica: *THES-uh-luh-NI-kuh*

Tirzah: *TIHR-zuh*

Titius Justus: *TISH-ee-uhs JUHS-tuhs*

Vashti: *VASH-ti*

Zacchaeus: *Za-KEE-uhs*

Zarephath: *ZAIR-uh-fath*

Zechariah: *ZEK-uh-RI-uh*

Zedekiah: *ZED-uh-KI-uh*

Zerubbabel: *Zuh-RUHB-uh-buhl*

Ziba: *ZI-buh*

Zophar: *ZOH-fahr*

Meet . . .
the Authors

Chrissie Muecke has a master's degree in elementary teaching and curriculum from the University of Rochester and is pursuing a master of arts in Christian leadership from Eastern Mennonite Seminary. She has worked for MennoMedia and Brethren Press as a curriculum writer and editor for 14 years. Chrissie co-authored three Bible storybooks titled *All of Us*, *All Together*, and *Great Big Love*. She attends Rochester (NY) Mennonite Fellowship.

Jasmin Pittman Morrell has a bachelor's degree in English, journalism, and creative writing from Berry College and a master of fine arts in narrative nonfiction writing from the University of Georgia. Her writing is featured in *Bigger Than Bravery* (2022) and other anthologies. Jasmin also supports "Family Voices," a creative writing mentorship program for children of color in Asheville, North Carolina. She believes deeply in radical hospitality and the holy power of the imagination.

Rev. Teresa Kim Pecinovsky holds a master of education from the University of Houston and a master of divinity from Vanderbilt Divinity School. She is an ordained minister through the Christian Church (Disciples of Christ). Teresa is the author of the children's book *Mother God* and works as a hospice chaplain. She lives in Houston, Texas, with her family and co-leads the pastoral care team at Houston Mennonite Church.

the Theological Advisors

Joan L. Daggett is the project director for *Shine: Living in God's Light*. She holds a master of arts in theology from Bethany Theological Seminary. An ordained minister in the Church of the Brethren, she has served in pastoral and judicatory ministries. Before coming to Shine, she served as executive director of the Brethren-Mennonite Heritage Center in Harrisonburg, Virginia.

Rev. Andrea De Avila is an associate pastor at Sargent Avenue Mennonite Church in Winnipeg, Manitoba. She holds a master in theological studies from Canadian Mennonite University. Andrea is also an alumna of Eastern Mennonite University and Hesston College. She is committed to volunteer work and currently serves with Mennonite Central Committee thrift shops and Mennonite Church Canada.

Carmen Brubacher lives, works, plays, and worships on the ancestral lands of the Anishnaabeg, Haudenosaunee, and Chonnonton peoples. She received a master of divinity degree from Anabaptist Mennonite Biblical Seminary and is the minister for faith formation at Waterloo North Mennonite Church in Waterloo, Ontario. Her family includes her husband and four teenage and young adult children.

Malinda Elizabeth Berry (PhD, Union Theological Seminary in the city of New York) is associate professor of theology and ethics and director of the Faith Formation Collaborative at Anabaptist Mennonite Biblical Seminary in Elkhart, Indiana. She is a peace theologian who is passionate about sharing Anabaptist-Mennonite perspectives on Christian living in a spirit of ecumenism while incorporating restorative practices from other traditions into her own. Her family is part of Faith Mennonite Church in Goshen, Indiana.

Rev. Sarah Ann Bixler (PhD, Princeton Theological Seminary) is assistant professor of formation and practical theology and associate dean at Eastern Mennonite Seminary in Harrisonburg, Virginia. Her scholarship focuses on adolescent formation and practices of attachment in Anabaptist faith communities. She, her spouse, and their three children attend Park View Mennonite Church.

the Illustration Consultants

Andrea Hill Fitzgerald (*see Meet the Illustrators*)

Jessie Houff is a multimedia artist currently living in Baltimore, Maryland. Jessie grew up with values rooted in family, travel, and spirituality. She received her master of fine art in community art and is the community arts minister at the Washington City Church of the Brethren, community arts coordinator at Wesley Theological Seminary (WTS), and adjunct professor at WTS in Washington, DC.

Teresa Kim Pecinovsky (*see Meet the Authors*)

the Illustrators

Alma Miller-Glick graduated in 2015 from Goshen College with a degree in PreK–12 art education and a certificate in peace, justice, and conflict studies. She currently resides in Lancaster, Pennsylvania, where she works as an illustrator and stay-at-home parent.

(*See pages 66–73, 256–259, 294–299.*)

Andrea Hill Fitzgerald is a Chicago-based artist, illustrator, and art educator who uses portraiture to address identity, race, class, and gender. Born in Louisville, Kentucky, Andrea began teaching Saturday art classes at the JB Speed Art museum at the age of 14. This cemented her love of making and teaching art. Andrea has art degrees from the Art Academy of Cincinnati and the University of Cincinnati College of Design, Architecture, Art, and Planning.

(*See pages 98–99, 176–181, 228–233.*)

Brian Dumm is an award-winning artist and educator from Pennsylvania. Working professionally since 2000, he has had his work featured throughout the United States in publications and exhibitions.

(*See pages 90–95, 134–135.*)

Cathy Morrison has illustrated and written over 40 children's books and is passionate about nature, science, and the environment. Cathy's studio is in the foothills of Fort Collins in Glacier View Meadows with a panoramic view of Rocky Mountain National Park. She enjoys hiking, gardening, and traveling.

(*See pages 122–133.*)

Clarissa Martinez is an illustrator and painter from Brownsville, Texas, where she is also an adjunct instructor at Texas Southmost College. She likes to use Adobe Photoshop, watercolors, oil paints, and ink to tell stories in her illustrations. She also dabbles in book making and animation.

(*See pages 74–77, 220–223.*)

Dave Huth is a teacher, storyteller, picture maker, nature photographer, and whistler of jaunty tunes. He works as a professor of visual communication and media arts at Houghton University in western New York state.

(*See pages 42–47, 106–107.*)

Elizabeth Erazo Baez is an artist, illustrator, curator, and art teacher. She has a bachelor of arts in art education from Florida International University. Through her art, she lives as an agent for community change dedicated to service, cultural preservation, and advancement of Puerto Rican art across the globe.

(*See pages 234–235.*)

Erin Bennett Banks has illustrated several children's books, including *The Celebration Place*, *Hush Harbor*, and *The Patchwork Path*. She has been recognized by *The New York Times*, Oppenheim Toy Portfolio, Jerry Pinkney Children's Book Award, and the Gustavus Myers Center for the Study of Bigotry and Human Rights. Erin lives in Charleston, South Carolina, with her illustrator husband and three girls.

(*See cover and pages 20–23, 136–139, 226–227, 330–334.*)

Fátima Anaya was born in El Salvador and received her bachelor's degree in graphic design at Don Bosco University in El Salvador. She combines illustration and graphic design. Her inspiration comes from love, peace, childhood, and historical events. She currently lives in San Salvador.

(*See pages 78–85.*)

Gabhor Utomo was born in Indonesia and moved to California to pursue his passion in art. He received his degree from the Academy of Art University in San Francisco. He has since worked as a freelance illustrator and illustrated several children's books, including *Kai's Journey to Gold Mountain*. Gabhor's work has won numerous awards from local and national art organizations. Gabhor lives with his wife Dina and his twin girls in Portland, Oregon.

(*See pages 190–191, 240–241.*)

Gina Capaldi studied fine arts at Pepperdine University and Pitzer College, and illustration at Art Center: College of Design. Gina has written and illustrated over 100 books and products for children that range from trade to educational, nonfiction, and merchandise. She often combines traditional painting techniques and mediums with collage and/or digital elements to add additional layers of visual storytelling. She lives in San Dimas, California.

(*See pages 244–245, 290–293.*)

Gwen Stamm has been drawing ever since she can remember. She studied primarily under art professors Bob Regier and Paul Friesen at Hesston and Bethel (Kansas) Colleges. She has worked and played as a graphic designer, illustrator, and calligrapher. In 2021, Gwen illustrated and self-published a book for children titled *Blessings Flow*.

(*See pages 24–25, 140–143.*)

Jesse Graber has degrees from Bethel College and the American Academy of Art in Chicago, Illinois. His illustrations have appeared in books, magazines, and websites across the world. He teaches art at Washington High School in Kansas City, Kansas, where he lives with his wife and their cats, Ruth, Pepper, and Jo Jo.

(*See pages 306–307, 312–315, 369.*)

Joani Rothenberg is an Indianapolis-based fine artist whose work includes illustrations, Judaica art, murals, and landscape paintings. She is also a board-certified art therapist. Her books include *Creation's First Light*, *Butterflies Under Our Hats*, *My First Siddur*, *Shabbat Angels*, and *Adam and Eve's First Sunset*.

(See pages 62–65.)

Joanne Robertson is Bald Eagle Clan, and her communities are Atikameksheng, Essex County, and Algoma, all in Ontario, Turtle Island. She earned her degree in fine arts from Algoma University and Shingwauk Kinoomaage Gamig in Bawating at age 50. Seven years later her first book, *Nibi Emosaawdang / The Water Walker*, about her teacher and friend Nokomis Josephine-ba Mandamin, was published by Second Story Press. She is currently working on a third book.

(See pages 236–237.)

Joy Keenan has illustrated many children's and young adult books, including *What Happens When Children Pray: Learning to Talk and Listen to God*, *Hemlock Hill Hideaway*, and *Nuestras Adventuras/Days of Adventure*. She lives on the Jersey Shore with her husband, Michael.

(See pages 208–209.)

Justine Maendel will graduate from Messiah University with a bachelor of fine arts degree in 2024. When she is not in school, she lives at the Foxhill Bruderhof Community in Montgomery, New York. As an artist, she loves figurative work in the form of both illustration and fine art and enjoys using a wide range of mediums including oils, watercolors, printmaking, dry media, and digital tools.

(See pages 108–117, 383.)

Kate Cosgrove is an award-winning children's book illustrator. Her latest picture book, *The Dirt Book: Poems About Animals that Live Beneath Our Feet*, was juried into the Original Art 41st Annual Exhibition in New York City and was a New York Public Library Best Book of the Year. She also illustrated *Maria's Kit of Comfort*. She lives with her family in a very old house in Michigan that is probably haunted.

(See pages 144–147, 162–175, 198–203, 210–211, 238–239, 242–243, 280–283, 316–325, 340–341, 345.)

LaTonya R. Jackson is a mother, educator, and author-illustrator. Her greatest wealth of inspiration comes from her son's quirky and wondrous views of the world. She enjoys creating stories that use textures to capture the multilayered lives of children of color. Her debut picture book, *Josey Johnson's Hair and the Holy Spirit*, is a 2022 Jerry Pinkney Children's Book Award Finalist. The book also earned the InterVarsity Press 2023 Readers' Choice Award in the Christian Living category.

(See pages 12, 100–105, 182–187, 250–255, 270–279.)

Laura James has been working as an artist for almost 30 years. Her African and Caribbean-American heritage, and a love of stories, design, and color, are all elements that have always been present in her work. She illustrated *The Book of the Gospels* lectionary as well as two children's books. Photo by Flordalis Espinal, used with permission.

(See pages 224–225.)

Laura Krushak-Tripp is an artist and children's illustrator. She lives in Utah with her husband and two young children. She graduated from Brigham Young University-Idaho where she focused on illustration. Her published works include illustrations for magazines, religious publications, and picture books, including *The Snow Baby* and *Growing in God's Love Story Bible*.

(See pages 34–41, 54–61.)

Linda (Piscia) Pierce has been illustrating for kids for more than 30 years. Her recent book is *Pippin No Drippin* by Layne Ihe. A graduate of Rhode Island School of Design, she also teaches art at Rock Hill Farm Studio, named for her grandparents' farm on which it sits.

(See pages 188–189, 204–205, 212–217, 246–247.)

Melanie Cataldo enjoys using pencil, oil, acrylic, and digital paint to build her illustrations. She has illustrated several children's books, including *Hiding Baby Moses*, *Home by Another Way*, and *The Stranded Whale*. She lives in central Massachusetts.

(See pages 284–289, 326–329.)

Michele Wood is an acclaimed artist, author, and mentor. The focus of her program is theology and the arts. She is a recipient of the Coretta Scott King Award, McCaw Scholarship, Global Ministry grant, and many others. Her children's books include *Like a Bird: The Art of the American Slave Song*, *I See the Rhythm*, *I Lay My Stitches Down*, *Chasing Freedom*, and *Going Back Home*. Her most recent illustrated book, *Box: Henry Brown Mails Himself to Freedom*, was a 2021 Newbery Honor Book.

(See pages 48–53, 300–305.)

Nathanael Eby has loved art since he was young. He attended art classes at St. Olaf College in Minnesota. He works as a freelance artist along with his other job and uses various mediums, such as drawing, digital art, painting, and woodworking. He currently lives in Harrisonburg, Virginia, and hopes to expand his work as an artist.

(See pages 118–121, 218–219.)

Ruth Goring grew up in Colombia and is a writer for children and a visual artist who works primarily in chalk pastels, collage, and mosaic. She wrote *Adriana's Angels* (available in English and Spanish) and *Isaiah and the Worry Pack*. Her author-illustrator debut is *Picturing God*, which invites children and parents to meditate on biblical metaphors for God.

(See pages 86–89, 148–157.)

Suling Wang loves playing with colors and light to create a mood or tell a story in her art. She lives in San Francisco, California, with her family and dog. Outside of work, she has a passion for food, cooking, learning new skills, martial arts, and gardening.

(See pages 26–33, 260–269.)

Tim Ladwig has illustrated more than 20 books, including *The Lord's Prayer* and *Psalm Twenty-Three*. He is a three-time Gold Medallion Award finalist and two-time American Booksellers Association "Pick of the Lists" award winner. He lives in Wichita, Kansas, with his wife. They have two daughters and a son.

(See pages 206–207, 308–311.)

Tom Barrett began professionally illustrating in 1972 and moved to Boston in 1978 to freelance illustrate for numerous publishers and advertising agencies. In 1983, he was invited to teach illustration at the Art Institute of Boston as an assistant professor and in 2000 taught at Massachusetts College of Art and Lesley University College of Art and Design. He now enjoys painting full time.

(*See pages 192–197.*)

Ying Hui Tan is a Malaysian illustrator from a small town in Perak. She enjoys storytelling. She aims to deliver love, happiness, and fun through her work by using shapes, colors, and movement. Her recent work is *Jade and the Clouds*, and she was blessed to illustrate the *New York Times* #1 Best Seller *What Is God Like?* by Rachel Held Evans and Matthew Paul Turner.

(*See pages 248–249.*)

"PEACE I LEAVE WITH YOU;
MY PEACE I GIVE TO YOU!"

—JESUS